Library Statistics:
A Handbook of
Concepts, Definitions, and Terminology

Library Statistics:

A *Handbook of*

Concepts, Definitions, and Terminology

Prepared by the Staff of the

Statistics Coordinating Project

Joel Williams, *Director*

American Library Association

Chicago, Illinois, 1966

Foreword

During the last half century, American libraries have gained recognition as essential partners in the educational community through their contribution to the educational process. As financial support from public and private sources increased, so did the requirements for improved evaluation and assessment of operational performance. Surveys and studies helped to raise libraries to a position from which the evaluation of their needs could lead to sound planning with regard to resources, personnel, and facilities. During the 1920's and 1930's the first studies were directed toward case study comparisons among institutions. The post World War II period, particularly the last ten years, saw a growing emphasis on area-wide surveys—local, state, regional, and national —dealing with all types of libraries. In these surveys, the statistical approach was frequently used because it provided quantitative expressions of observed phenomena, lent itself to descriptive and analytical purposes, and permitted projective conclusions.

The use of statistics in the behavioral and social sciences was occasionally questioned because close scrutiny indicated that data relating to one locality were combined with those of others where concepts differed. Undoubtedly, some surveys used incompatible combinations and made invalid comparisons which led to unreliable conclusions. To overcome these difficulties, researchers in various disciplines began to coordinate statistical accounting through the standardization of terms and the preparation of standard definitions. They proceeded on the assumption that uniformity would provide clarification for researcher and respondent alike and would result in comparable data.

Librarians have been aware of these problems and have been attempting corrective action for at least 20 years. Two landmarks in the recognition of these difficulties were a conference held in the U.S. Office of Education in 1946 and the publication of *Definitions for Library Statistics, a Preliminary Draft* in the late 1950's, the result of David C. Weber's work with the A.L.A.-L.A.D. Statistics Coordinating Committee. Preparation of the latter brought the lack of generally accepted statistical terms into sharper focus and made it obvious to the members of the L.A.D. Statistics Committee that the task would require a more detailed study than could be carried on through a committee with a constantly changing membership. In 1960 David H. Clift, Executive Director of the A.L.A., canvassed all divisions of the A.L.A. for specific proposals. In this connection, the Statistics Coordinating Committee, with G. Flint Purdy as Chairman, submitted a proposal for a National Survey of Library Statistics. This proposal presented a systematic approach for coordinating and unifying the national needs for library statistics.

During this same period, a parallel activity got under way in the S.L.A., and a Statistics Committee under the chairmanship of Ruth Fine was created. This group developed plans similar to A.L.A.'s for special libraries. For the purposes of this project Bill Woods, Executive Secretary of S.L.A., and Ruth Fine met during the Midwinter Meeting and the Annual A.L.A. Conference with the A.L.A.-L.A.D. Statistics Coordinating Committee to maintain liaison between the two associations.

By 1961, the A.L.A.-L.A.D. Statistics Coordinating Committee had developed a time schedule and a project proposal for presentation to the Council on Library Resources. During the 1962 A.L.A. Midwinter Meeting, the A.L.A. and S.L.A. projects were combined and various economies were agreed upon. In January 1963, the final proposal was accepted by the Council on Library Resources. During the developmental stages, the emphasis shifted from conducting a study of needs for, and uses of, library statistics, to the standardization of terms, definitions, and concepts for library statistics.

Through these years of planning and implementation of the project, Alphonse F. Trezza has coordinated the work. Close liaison was maintained with Verner Clapp and Melville Ruggles of the Council on Library Resources. Grateful acknowledgment is made of the basic Council grant, the supplemental grant from the National Science Foundation, and the provision of office space in the National Library of Medicine.

The project may be cited as a highly successful demonstration of cooperation among library associations, funding agencies, governmental and private organizations, and national and international bodies. It may well prove the basis for an international standard for library statistics, having been recognized by the International Federation of Library Associations at the August 1964 Rome Conference and by the International Standards Organization Technical Committee/46 during its October 1964 Budapest Conference. It is expected that a meeting of the Statistics Committees of these two organizations will prepare a working paper for such a standard and submit it to UNESCO for adoption as a UNESCO recommendation.

Only the uses to which this handbook will be put, and the periodic revisions it may receive, will accurately gauge its success. Considering the devotion of its staff, the contributions from the members of the supporting organizations (A.L.A.-L.A.D., S.L.A., ASA-Z39, and PNLA), and the assistance received from librarians in all types of libraries, the future for library statistics research looks most promising.

Frank L. Schick
Washington, D.C.

March, 1966

Preface

As of July 1, 1964, the A.L.A. Statistics Coordinating Project formally came to an end after one year of investigation of the field of library statistics. This Project had as its principal objectives the development of this handbook and the formulation of a comprehensive program for the systematic collection of statistics for all types of libraries. During the year of formal activity on the Project, the primary emphasis was focused upon the preparation of this handbook.

The staff of the Project comprised a full-time director and several consultant librarians who were employed part of the year to prepare the individual chapters related to statistics of specific types of libraries. The staff roster is as follows:

Director: Joel Williams, U.S. Office of Education, Washington, D.C.

Secretary: Cecilia Manstof

College and University Libraries: Marietta Chicorel, Ulrich's International Periodicals Index, New York City

Public and State Libraries: David Palmer, New Jersey State Library, Trenton

School Libraries: Richard Darling, Montgomery County School System, Rockville, Md.

Special Libraries: Anne McCann, National Library of Medicine, Washington, D.C.

Library Education: Sarah Reed, U.S. Office of Education

An Advisory Committee to the Project was also appointed, and maintained a continuing liaison with the Project's activities by means of periodic meetings throughout the year. This Advisory Committee was composed of the following members:

G. Flint Purdy (Chairman), Wayne State University
Henry J. Dubester, National Science Foundation
Eloise Q. Ebert, Oregon State Library
Ruth Fine, U.S. Bureau of the Budget
Harold S. Hacker, Rochester Public Library
Robert E. Kingery, New York Public Library
Melville J. Ruggles, Council on Library Resources, Inc.
Frank L. Schick, U.S. Office of Education
James M. Skipper, Association of College and Research
    Libraries
Alphonse F. Trezza, American Library Association

In order that this handbook represent the opinions and suggestions of widely diverse groups of librarians, not only geographically but also with respect to types of library and types of activity, the draft of the basic chapters of this handbook was quite thoroughly examined by more than 160 librarians in a series of four regional conferences held in Atlanta, San Francisco, Chicago, and New York City (see Appendix A). This handbook thus represents the distillation of the points of view of the statistics-oriented segment of the library profession.

At the same time, this publication represents only a beginning in the process of codification of concepts, definitions, and terminology. At this point, the handbook is intended (a) to isolate and describe those aspects of library activity which are measurable, (b) to define these characteristics with a precision that will eliminate confusion whenever a particular term is used, and (c) to propose the elimination of data which have outlived their usefulness, but continue to be collected because of tradition. The process of continuing research and revision must go on. Only through the universal implementation of this handbook can further progress be accomplished.

Joel Williams

Acknowledgments

Credit for writing the specific chapters should be accorded as follows:

Chapter I: Joel Williams, National Center for Educational Statistics, U.S. Office of Education, Washington, D.C.

Chapter II: Marietta Chicorel, Ulrich's International Periodicals Index, New York City. (Formerly at University of Washington Library, Seattle.)

Chapters III, IV: David Palmer, New Jersey State Library, Trenton. (Formerly at Pennsylvania State Library, Harrisburg.)

Chapter V: Richard L. Darling, Montgomery County School System, Rockville, Md. (Formerly at U.S. Office of Education, Washington, D.C.)

Chapter VI: Anne McCann, National Library of Medicine, Washington, D.C. (Formerly at American Pharmaceutical Association Library, Washington, D.C.)

Chapter VII: Sarah Reed, U.S. Office of Education, Washington, D.C.

Glossary: Joel Williams, National Center for Educational Statistics, U.S. Office of Education, Washington, D.C.

Contents

General Concepts

The principal objective of this handbook is the standardization of concepts, definitions, and terminology for the several basic types of libraries. In the development of the contents of the handbook, we have been mindful that libraries are keeping the many records and counts of their various activities and operations for a variety of purposes: evaluating the efficiency of the numerous operations within the library, reporting to management, justifying their budget requests, keeping the public at large (and their clientele in particular) apprised of their activities. But there are other reasons for keeping many of these records—reasons that transcend their use and meaning within the confines of an individual library. Meaning can be imparted to certain data only when they are compared from library to library, when they are summarized into indexes, averages, or ratios for groupings of similar libraries, or when selected measurements are compared with predetermined standards. Also, it is only through the use of valid data that standards, many of which have been arbitrarily determined, can be revised and made more meaningful.

The format of the handbook changed several times during the period the Project was in existence. Numerous factors were instrumental in this "evolutionary" process, not the least of which was the limitation of time and staff and the fact that in every Project certain initial hypotheses result in "blind alleys." After some false starts, we decided upon the approach of concentrating on a discussion of statistics as they relate to the major types of libraries. Of course, in so doing, type-of-activity areas per se have not been discussed.

The chapters were subjected to careful scrutiny, not only by the Advisory Committee but by numerous other consultants as well. We then submitted the manuscript to thorough examination at four regional meetings attended by a complete cross-section of the library profession. About 165 librarians attended these regional meetings. (See Appendix A.)

The handbook is intended (1) to isolate and describe those aspects of library activity which are measurable, i.e., can be expressed in numerical terms, (2) to define these characteristics with a precision that will eliminate confusion whenever a particular term is used, and (3) to propose the elimination of certain measures which have outlived their usefulness but continue to be collected because of tradition. To allay numerous misunderstandings, the following statements indicate what the handbook is *not* designed to accomplish:

> The handbook does not set standards of library service, resources, or facilities, nor does it develop measures of quality.
>
> The handbook does not present any statistics for libraries. We have conducted no statistical studies nor have we compiled data from other sources for presentation in the handbook.
>
> The handbook does not contain specific examples of questionnaires which can be used without alteration or pretesting for the several types of libraries.
>
> The handbook does not attempt to describe or explore all aspects of a library's program. In a number of instances, however, special studies are recommended for particular aspects of the program.
>
> The handbook does not propose a national program of library statistics, nor does it contain recommendations for statistical analysis of library programs.
>
> The handbook does not deal specifically with statistics that cut across all libraries, that is, type-of-activity functions such as library manpower, technical services, reference services, young adults' and children's services, and the like.

How far we have gone in achieving our major objectives only time will tell. It is readily apparent that the handbook will not answer all questions nor solve all problems in the field of library statistics, but we hope that it can, even at present, provide the essential elements, or "building blocks," necessary for the construction of questionnaires to be used in the conduct of statistical surveys of libraries. As special investigations are completed in problem areas, the handbook can incorporate their findings.

In isolating and describing quantitative factors for statistical analysis, we are, in effect, defining them. When these factors become the units on which libraries can agree, they are then the comparable units on which survey questionnaires can be based, be they for internal or external use. Comparability is one controlling measure, feasibility the other. Much of the research being carried out today loses its true value because we can draw no valid inferences and develop no generalizations from the data. Other needed research is not being performed for lack of a base from which to proceed. Because we can not foresee all of the uses researchers, administrators, legislators, or commercial enterprises wish to make of these data, statistical units should be broad enough to have wide applicability, yet specific enough to remain meaningful.

Standard Measures

In the initial planning of this handbook, we had assumed that the various types of libraries had enough basic similarities to permit evaluating and describing them in a single chapter, thus reserving for the several types of libraries only a discussion of their unique characteristics. As our investigations developed, it was discovered that these basic similarities were apparently subject to numerous exceptions and could be described more efficiently in separate chapters. Although we have maintained this approach in the handbook, a post-audit, as it were, reveals that differences among libraries, by type, are not as widespread as we had assumed, especially with respect to basic characteristics.

The table "Counts of Basic Characteristics" represents a summary of recommendations for maintaining counts of basic characteristics by the major types of libraries. You will note that at times a different approach is recommended for some types of libraries. By referring to the specific chapters for these libraries, you will be able to find explanations for the deviation.

Surveys and Sample Studies

The technique of developing and designing good sample surveys has become so standard in the past 25 years that it would

Counts of Basic Characteristics

(Items included in the table indicate
how they are to be counted when a count is required)

Item	College and University	Public	State	School	Special
Book Stock					
Volumes at beginning of year	Yes	Yes	Yes	Yes	Yes
Volumes added	Yes	Yes	Yes	Yes	Yes
Volumes withdrawn	Yes	Yes	Yes	Yes	Yes
Volumes at end of year	Yes	Yes	Yes	Yes	Yes
Titles added	No	Yes	Yes	No	Yes
Periodicals					
Bound—by bibliographic volume	No	Yes	Yes	Yes	Yes
Unbound—by bibliographic volume	Yes	Yes	Yes	Yes	Yes
Current subscriptions by item	Yes	No	No	No	No
Current subscriptions by title	Yes	Yes	Yes	Yes	Yes
Microform					
Include with other holdings, by type	No	Yes	Yes	Yes*	No
Count separately by physical item	Yes	Yes	Yes	Yes	Yes
Nonbook Materials					
Itemized materials counted by item	Yes	Yes	Yes	Yes	Yes
Vertical file material by linear feet	No	Yes	Yes	No	Yes
Circulation					
Direct circulation	No	Yes	Yes	No	Yes
Interlibrary loan (lent and borrowed)	Yes	Yes	Yes	No	Yes
Photocopies in lieu of circulation	No	Yes	Yes	No	Yes
Reference					
Number of transactions	No	Yes	Yes	No	Yes
Personnel					
Number of filled & vacant positions, by type	Yes	Yes	Yes	Yes	Yes
Salaries of full-time professional staff	Yes	Yes	Yes	Yes	Yes
Financial Data					
Income by source	No	Yes	Yes	No	No
Expenditure by type	Yes	Yes	Yes	Yes	Yes
Physical Facilities					
Area in square feet	Yes	Yes	Yes	Yes	Yes
Seating capacity	Yes	Yes	Yes	Yes	Yes
Shelf capacity	Yes	Yes	Yes	Yes	Yes

*For periodicals only.

not be worthwhile to engage in a detailed description of procedures and mathematical proofs. There are many experts available for consultation when the need arises. It would be more profitable, then, to indicate the general principles involved in determining when a sample survey is feasible. Basically, the decision depends on the following factors:

Timeliness—How quickly must the data be available in order to be useful?

Cost—How much can we afford to spend for these data?

Precision—How much error can we tolerate in the final results; that is, would we arrive at the same conclusions and make the same decisions had we used all possible respondents?

Detail—How useful will these data be if available only for the nation? or by region? or by state?

Once a decision has been reached on the basis of the foregoing principles, what is needed in order to conduct an adequate sample survey? First, we must have a complete "universe" of the respondents whom we would canvass if we were conducting our survey on a complete basis. Second, we must maintain strict controls of the probabilities in the selection of our sample in order to be able to indicate the precision of the estimates which result. And third, we must obtain an adequate reply from all respondents in the sample.[1]

When all of these conditions have been met, the processing, inflation, and presentation of the sample data, as well as computations revealing the reliability of the data, are quite straightforward. There is no implication here that the process is simple but merely that sampling techniques have been developed to such an extent that the services of specialists in this area are readily obtainable.

The importance of sampling techniques cannot be stressed enough, especially in the area of national statistical aggregates, because the several major types of libraries are quite numerous and they are increasing in number. Although some might argue that the total number of college and university libraries (about 2,000) is reasonably small enough for a complete canvass, this argument loses its validity in the case of the 8,000 public libraries, the 8,000 special libraries, and the more than 50,000 school

---

[1]It is recognized that there are special techniques that can be used for subsampling the nonrespondent group if necessary.

libraries. The multiplicity of surveys and research studies now being conducted makes it imperative that all persons involved in the collection of library statistics conduct a searching inquiry into their basic requirements with a view toward minimizing the number of respondents, as well as the volume of data to be collected and processed.

Another factor which must be discussed in this connection is the amount of detail that is required and the variation in the amount of this detail depending upon the need. In some instances, only a single figure is needed for the nation as a whole, as in the case of total operating expenditures for college and university libraries. On the other hand, the U.S. Office of Education annually publishes quite detailed statistics for each college and university library, so that an individual librarian is able to analyze patterns of operation in libraries comparable with his own in size and organization. Obviously, both types can be justified; but only with a well-planned and well-executed statistical program in operation can we hope to obtain both in an efficient manner. One can visualize an annual sample survey which will produce basic national data, plus a complete quadrennial canvass for the purpose of providing new benchmarks for the sample, as well as allowing libraries to compare themselves with their "neighbors." Of course, this is merely a single illustration. A great many factors would have to be coordinated before a final program could be developed.

Library Universes

In the conduct of statistical surveys of libraries, it is of utmost importance that the person conducting the survey delimit the group of libraries to which he will address his questionnaire. Traditionally, libraries have been subdivided for survey purposes into several major groups, namely, public, school, college and university, and special. In this Project we have examined statistics for these several groups very carefully, and in the chapters that follow, statistics for the particular groups are analyzed in depth. In addition, we have added a chapter on State Library Agencies, which have been subject to very few statistical compilations in the past.

However, it has become apparent that classification of libraries into only a few broad groupings is not sufficient for statistical purposes. Also, it is evident that large groups of libraries are being omitted from the statistical picture because they cannot be classified into one or the other of these few major groups. A more precise examination of the classification of libraries for statistical purposes is needed, as well as the establishment of criteria that are specific enough to classify the library into one group or another. Obviously, it is virtually impossible to set criteria that are definitive enough to insure that a library will be classified uniquely. For example, under one set of criteria the New York Public Library is a public library, but many of its subject departments can also be classified as special libraries. Then, too, there are other groupings of libraries, such as the "Research Libraries," which overlap several of the traditional groupings.

Studies of groupings of "specialized" libraries have not been considered by this Project. Our concern is to stress the fact that mutually exclusive groupings of libraries must be specifically determined in order that statistical studies may be carried out for these particular types of libraries. It is vital that all libraries falling into a particular group be accurately identified, so that they may be surveyed in any study concerning their group.

In addition to the basic types of libraries already mentioned, the following libraries must be considered as discrete groups in any overall and national inventory of library resources:

Libraries connected with religious organizations, such as the many Catholic parish libraries in the United States.

Base libraries for the use of military personnel.

Patient and inmate libraries in hospitals and correctional institutions.

Association and labor-union libraries for the use of members.

Although these libraries do not qualify for inclusion in the basic types of libraries mentioned above, they must be considered in the evaluation of total library resources in the United States. Also, when one is evaluating library use and library resources on a national basis, it is readily apparent that libraries of this type will have an impact on the statistics.

An examination of the commonality of use and service of the libraries in the list above discloses that their clientele represents specialized groups of the general public. It is therefore possible to classify these libraries as subgroups of public libraries, and the chapter dealing with the statistics of public libraries may be applicable to them. Note that special mention was made of the clientele of these libraries. There are also professional libraries located within these institutions, and these should be classified as special libraries. In some cases, it is very difficult to separate the two since both types of clientele may be using the same facilities, often with a single professional librarian supervising both types of activities. However, since the functions of both parts are so basically different, it is extremely important in the collection of statistics of libraries by type that these two functions be separated to the best of the respondent's ability.

Library Organization

In the general texts which deal with the library and its organization, one can include all of the activities of the library, regardless of type, within one of three general areas. These are (1) Administration, (2) Readers' Services, (3) Technical Services.

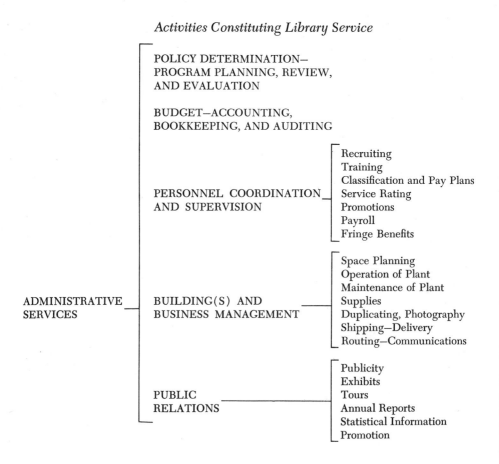

Activities Constituting Library Service

POLICY DETERMINATION—
PROGRAM PLANNING, REVIEW,
AND EVALUATION

BUDGET—ACCOUNTING,
BOOKKEEPING, AND AUDITING

PERSONNEL COORDINATION
AND SUPERVISION
- Recruiting
- Training
- Classification and Pay Plans
- Service Rating
- Promotions
- Payroll
- Fringe Benefits

ADMINISTRATIVE
SERVICES

BUILDING(S) AND
BUSINESS MANAGEMENT
- Space Planning
- Operation of Plant
- Maintenance of Plant
- Supplies
- Duplicating, Photography
- Shipping—Delivery
- Routing—Communications

PUBLIC
RELATIONS
- Publicity
- Exhibits
- Tours
- Annual Reports
- Statistical Information
- Promotion

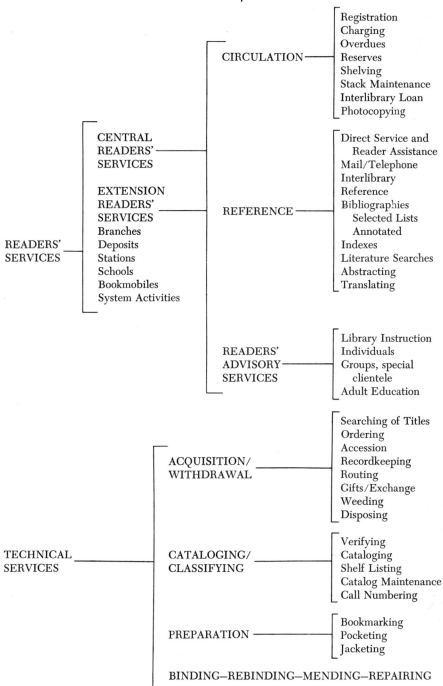

READERS' SERVICES

CENTRAL READERS' SERVICES

EXTENSION READERS' SERVICES
Branches
Deposits
Stations
Schools
Bookmobiles
System Activities

CIRCULATION
- Registration
- Charging
- Overdues
- Reserves
- Shelving
- Stack Maintenance
- Interlibrary Loan
- Photocopying

REFERENCE
- Direct Service and Reader Assistance
- Mail/Telephone
- Interlibrary
- Reference
- Bibliographies
- Selected Lists
- Annotated
- Indexes
- Literature Searches
- Abstracting
- Translating

READERS' ADVISORY SERVICES
- Library Instruction
- Individuals
- Groups, special clientele
- Adult Education

TECHNICAL SERVICES

ACQUISITION/ WITHDRAWAL
- Searching of Titles
- Ordering
- Accession
- Recordkeeping
- Routing
- Gifts/Exchange
- Weeding
- Disposing

CATALOGING/ CLASSIFYING
- Verifying
- Cataloging
- Shelf Listing
- Catalog Maintenance
- Call Numbering

PREPARATION
- Bookmarking
- Pocketing
- Jacketing

BINDING—REBINDING—MENDING—REPAIRING

The first is concerned with policy and planning functions, personnel, buildings and equipment, records and reports, finance, and supplies and equipment. The second deals with the clientele in a direct service and teaching function. The third includes the activities inherent in obtaining and organizing library materials for use. Although the terminology used in describing each of these activities may differ among the various types of libraries, in general it will be possible to classify all of the activities of the library within this framework. The "Activities" chart represents the general approach to outlining specific functions carried on within each of the three major groupings.

In the chapters of this handbook which deal with the various types of libraries, an attempt has been made generally to follow this pattern. Of course, with respect to the collection of statistics, it has not been possible to deal specifically with each activity listed on the extreme right. The problem that arises is the method by which these items, taken singly or in groups, can be evaluated not only within a given library but also between libraries, with respect to quantity and quality. Over a period of many years, libraries have developed a traditional list of items for which data have been reported. These data have been duly summarized year after year and submitted to boards of directors. Only in rare instances have the data been evaluated and only in rare instances has anyone dared to propose that an item be dropped from the list. These benchmark items have been examined with a view toward eliminating those which have outlived their usefulness, and new ones added to assist in the evaluation of library services. For example, in the chapter on public-library statistics, it is suggested that national data not be collected on registration, but that sample surveys in depth be conducted periodically to evaluate registration policies and procedures. The other chapters generally recommend that the periodicals collection be reported in terms of a count of "bibliographic" volumes. In both instances, there has been some objection from members of the library profession because of the fact that we are flaunting tradition. We are well aware that any suggested change might represent a substantial effort by librarians in altering their methods of maintaining their accounts or of counting their holdings.

Definitions and Terminology

The *Glossary of Terms Used in Statistical Surveys* in this handbook deserves some special mention and explanation. In any statistical survey program, the stabilization of terminology and the standardization of definitions are of primary importance in the data-collection process. In effect, we are establishing a common language to be used when the information is being generated, when it is being compiled from numerous sources, and finally when it is being analyzed and interpreted by the user. Through the use of this common language, comparability can be maintained at a local, state, and federal level among the many varied items of information required for evaluating library resources and performance.

This glossary is a product of many sources and many minds. Naturally, certain basic general glossaries in the field of librarianship were used as foundations for the present listing of terms. Only those terms which would have relevance to material in the handbook were selected for definition. In effect, then, the glossary is highly limited and specialized, as its title implies. It developed as the handbook developed and was revised and edited as the chapters were changed. It was probably examined more closely and more carefully than any other part of the handbook. Despite this close scrutiny, it will be out of date sooner than the rest of this handbook.

II

Statistics of
College and University
Libraries

In this chapter, those measurements which are unique to college and university libraries were considered from the point of view of their significance for national statistical reports. In this respect, recommendations that certain data be excluded are as important as those for data which should be included.

Summary statistics are useful for comparison of national, regional, and state resources; they provide a factual basis for the development of standards. While a standardized approach to reporting has been of prime concern, consideration has also been given to current local institutional practices.

When reporting college and university library statistics, the limits of areas to be reported should be defined. In its statistics, the central library should report (1) the central library collections and the branch and departmental library collections housed in the central library building, (2) all branch and departmental libraries located on the same campus but physically separate from the central library, and (3) extension center libraries located off campus. Libraries located off campus at instructional centers which do not constitute a *separate* campus should also be included in the central library's report, even in those cases where the name used to describe the library is neither "branch" nor "extension center library." "Number of branches" in the library system should not include departmental library collections in the central library building. Information on "Number of branches" should be reported in relation to statistics on physical facilities. The library system, which comprises those library facilities under the administration of the director of the central library, should be reported as one subtotal of the grand total of the institution's report on library activities. Autonomous libraries located on the same campus as the central library and libraries located on separate campuses should also be reported as separate subtotals and included in the grand total of the institution's statistical report.

Collections of books which do not qualify as a library (see glossary), such as in the office of the Head of a Department or in a science laboratory, are not to be included in the institution's report, even if the acquisition and processing of books are handled by the library staff.

Organization

The college or university library organization may be thought of as a threefold division of managerial responsibility: (1) *Administration,* which is concerned with policy and planning functions, personnel, buildings and equipment, records and reports, finance, and supplies and equipment;[1] (2) *Readers' Services,* which deals with the clientele in a direct service and teaching function; and (3) *Technical Services* which are concerned with the activities inherent in obtaining and organizing library materials for use.[2]

The following description of divisional responsibility is intended to be functional and general. It is recognized that there are many internal variations but these should not affect the general discussion.

Administration. Administration includes planning, organizing, staffing, directing, coordinating, reporting, and budgeting.[3] These are certainly the elements of administration, but there are also activities under this grouping which may overlap the divisional responsibilities of Technical Services and Readers' Services, and others which cover activities performed for the library system. These include:

---

[1]Louis Round Wilson and Maurice F. Tauber, *The University Library* (2nd ed.; New York: Columbia University Press, 1956), pp. 114-157.

[2]James Skipper, "The Present and Future Development of Technical Services," *Library Resources & Technical Services,* VI, No. 3 (Summer, 1962), 205.

[3]Louis Round Wilson and Maurice F. Tauber, *The University Library* (2nd ed.; New York: Columbia University Press, 1956).

Personnel for the library system
Mail receipts, sorting, and delivery for the
    library system
Building and equipment
Photoduplication
Maintenance

Readers' Services. Again a caution seems indicated. The grouping of specific activities and services under Readers' Services
does not constitute a recommendation for their internal administrative organization, but a guidepost for use in interinstitutional
comparison. "In its most comprehensive aspects and on a theoretical basis a coordinated readers' department would include
all units which serve the reader or circulate materials."[3] They
are suggested as follows:

Circulation
Stack control
Reference
Interlibrary loan
Reserve Book Room
Periodicals
Special collections (manuscripts,
    rare books, newspapers,
    microfilm, documents)
Library extension

Technical Services. In 1955 Felix Reichman wrote, "In keeping
with the thoroughly individualistic nature of these institutions
[large research libraries] there is a great diversity as to the place
of the [acquisitions] department in the general library structure;
a similar heterogeneity can be found in the definition of its function and duties."[4]

The same thing can be said today of Technical Services, of
which the organization of acquisitions departments is the most
fluid and varied. Groupings which would fall into a pattern
called Technical Services may be made if a Technical Service
definition is available to be followed. Whether or not library divisions are actually organized this way, they can certainly be
thought of as follows:

---

[4]Felix Reichman, "Management and Operation," *Library Trends,* III, No. 4
(April, 1955), 462.

Acquisitions:
  Selection
  Bibliographic searching
  Precataloging
  Ordering
  Gifts and exchanges
  Binding preparation and mendery
  Binding
Cataloging:
  Catalog preparation
  Classification
  Book preparation
  Catalog maintenance
  Making acquisitions lists
  Card reproduction
  Card preparation

Control and Type of Institution

RECOMMENDATIONS

1 *List public or private control.*

It is recommended that the present distinction between public and private control now observed by the U.S. Office of Education in its reporting for institutions of higher education be continued for college and university libraries. This distinction gives some indication of the funding of the library operation, its eligibility for state and federal support, and the scope of its potential clientele.

2 *Indicate type of institution.*

In order to make institutions distinguishable by type without the necessity of recourse to other publications, summary tabulations should be presented by type of institution, that is, university, liberal arts college, teachers college, technological school, theological or religious school, other professional school, and junior college. Tabulations of data for institutions by control and type facilitate comparisons within homogeneous groupings.

Population Served

RECOMMENDATIONS

1 *List number of teaching and research faculty, full-time and part-time separately.*

Inclusion of the teaching and research faculty as part of the library's clientele seems both mandatory and feasible. The number of faculty members should be reported in terms of number of full-time and number of part-time faculty in order to make them comparable. If reports of full-time equivalents (FTE) could be obtained nationally, based on an agreed-upon standard for "full-time," full- and part-time data could be consolidated into a single figure. As it is, such figures are not now obtainable. An argument has been advanced that the collection of data for both faculty and students was not necessary because of a relatively constant faculty-student ratio. It is, however, important to obtain data on the totality of the population served by college and university libraries because of the many uses to which this figure is put in the computation of derived statistics, such as per capita expenditures. Also, as a distinct group of users, faculty members serve as an indicator of the research function of the library. This definition of clientele is not limited to teaching and research faculty, but includes professional library and professional administrative faculty of an institution as well as all service personnel on campus who have academic status. It should be identical with the definition used by the U.S. Office of Education in its publication *Faculty and Other Professional Staff in Institutions of Higher Education. First Term 1959-1960, U.S. Office of Education.*

2 *List student enrollment, full-time and part-time separately.*

Student enrollment should be reported separately for full-time and for part-time students, on campus or in extension centers, both in programs which are creditable toward bachelor's or higher degrees and in programs which are not, i.e., programs of general studies and "terminal-occupational" programs. Separate campuses should be reported separately. Full- and part-time enrollment should not be totaled, since such a figure is misleading when related to library use or seating capacity.

3 *List number of graduate students.*

The number of graduate students is an important factor related to expenditures for library materials ".... the [N.Y. State Education] Department estimates the cost for good library service to college undergraduates at about $50.00 per person annually. 'It is estimated that the cost for good library service to graduate students is about $500 (per person) annually. This is because they need a far greater variety of books, and many books which are rare and expensive.' "[5] The number of graduate students, as related to total users, is also indicative of the impact of research activities on the library.

4 *Omit nonacademic employees.*

Another segment of potential users of the university or college library is composed of all nonacademic employees of the institution. It is recommended that reporting of this segment be omitted, because it does not significantly influence any part of the library's planning and operation.

Hours of Service
RECOMMENDATION

Omit for national reporting.

The amount of time the library is open and the amount of time the library is open-and-staffed are not necessarily identical. Hours open may differ considerably between departmental libraries and the central library; and while 84 hours per week is the estimated average time during which college and university libraries are open, the range is from 70 to 120 hours. Although this information is of inherent interest, it is of statistical value only in a special study directed at practices in college and university library administration. The cross-classification of data on hours open with the amount and type of service available, the type of staffing available, and the particular period during which the library is open (evening, week-end, etc.), for the central library and branch libraries separately, can provide useful detail for the evaluation of hours of service as they affect library performance standards.

It is therefore recommended that hours of service not be reported in national recurring surveys.

Library Holdings

As a factor in the determination of the size of the library, library holdings represent the static picture, whereas current acquisitions give the dynamic picture of the library. Annual reporting of holdings shows where the institution stands, while

---

[5]*Knowledge Is Power* (rev. ed.; Albany: N.Y. State Education Department, 1962). Quoted in Harold Bloomquist, "The Status and Needs of Medical Libraries in the United States," *Journal of Medical Education* (March, 1963), 38:145-163.

"volumes added" gives insight into how it got there. For national statistical use, certain categories are essential. Books, monographic serials, and periodical publications should be reported as one total by physical volumes, microfilm in terms of reels, and microcard and microfiche in terms of single physical unit; current subscriptions should be reported by total number of subscriptions as well as by number of titles. Volumes, reels, microcards, and microfiche should be reported annually in terms of the number of each added and withdrawn during the fiscal year, as well as the total held in each category at the beginning and the end of that fiscal year.

RECOMMENDATIONS

1 *Report physical volume count of items which fit the definition.*

To determine the holdings of a library, a physical volume count should be reported according to the definition of a volume (see glossary). Books, monographic serials, and periodical publications should be reported in the total count of volumes held at the end of the reporting year. Theses are included in the volume definition, as are appropriate government documents and technical reports.

2 *Omit title count.*

It is recommended that "titles added" not be reported nationally. The "titles added" count does not add significant information because it is in essence a cataloging count. It represents only the titles cataloged during the reporting period, not those added to the collections "ready for use" by some other means (such as by inserting a temporary slip in the main card catalog from the manifold order form). "Titles added" may represent in part the cataloging backlog, i.e., titles which were cataloged during the reporting year but were added in previous years.

Total number of titles in the collection could be cited as a check on total volumes held, if both were reported. However, there is some doubt about the validity and worth of such data. The points in favor of adding a title count to the physical count are (*a*) that it would balance the count where long runs of serials and duplicate copies of books tend to distort the volume count; (*b*) that it would give some insight into the title-to-volume ratio.

The arguments against a title count in addition to volume count are (*a*) that it cannot be done by measuring the shelf list, because cataloging practice varies in respect to multiple copies, which may be on separate shelf-list cards in some libraries and on one card in others, thereby negating the purpose of the title count; cataloging practice varies also in regard to title analytics made, so that some series may be analyzed this way, and others not; (*b*) that annual totals after the initial count must be made by either continuing to measure the shelf list each year or by adding titles cataloged during the year cumulatively (neither choice has proven satisfactory); (*c*) that too many columns of varying statistics are confusing rather than helpful to the user; (*d*) that no statistics should be included which clearly do not contribute to particular needs.

3 *Count total current subscriptions (including government serials[6]) and also subscriptions by title count.*

Current subscriptions should include all periodical and serial subscriptions, including newspapers. Total current subscriptions, including duplicates reflect a library's acquisitions program in relation to its expenditures for library materials and in relation to use, and is consistent with the physical volume count. A subsection, listing number of titles subscribed to, shows depth of coverage and should also be reported.

Service-based subscriptions and monographs received in series will fall into the subscription count, but it is recommended that serially received monographs be included separately in the volume count.[7]

4 *Count unbound periodicals by bibliographic volume, but list separately from total volume count. Report only if this category represents an appreciable segment of the collection.*

Unbound periodicals should be counted by bibliographic volume, that is, by publisher's volume. Because a number of libraries refrain from binding extensive periodical holdings for reasons of economy and practicability for circulation, these resources would

---

[6] A government publication should be counted with serial subscriptions if it is identified as a periodical in the February issue of the *U.S. Government Monthly Catalog*.

[7] Recommendation made by the Association of Southeastern Research Libraries Statistics Committee, January 29, 1960.

otherwise go unreported. The opportunity should exist to list unbound periodicals as a separate category from the physical volume count of holdings.

5 *Microform:*
    a) Count microfilm holdings by reel, as separate total.
    b) Count microfiche and microcard by card, as separate total.

Microform is regarded as a separate significant category of holdings. It falls into two broad categories—reels and sheet forms. Although both physical volume and microform share a common role as information sources, it is recognized that accessibility and cost factors add significant differences in terms of library holdings. Microform represents a format which is less accessible to users than the printed book because its use is limited by the necessary physical equipment, such as micro-readers. It is valuable in locating specific information known to the user, but it is less useful for searching information through indexes, tables of contents, and chapters with the intent of finding needed material instantly. Microfilm in academic libraries is used to reduce storage space required for newspapers and to replace or acquire out-of-print books and periodicals. It is usually of most use in areas where repeated access by many people is not of the highest importance. The more recently established the library is, the more out-of-print material it may lack, which it will probably purchase in microfilm form.

In a number of libraries, particularly the smaller ones, the request for a report of microform holdings in terms of volumes or titles, rather than reels, would result in noncomparability because of differences in counting methods. The situation is aggravated in some cases where small spools of microfilm have been spliced together and each article or part of an article is counted as a separate bibliographic unit. In these cases, we can present a fair picture to the library-user as well as the administrator by consistently reporting total holdings of libraries in terms of physical units.

Because of these differences, it is recommended that the volume count and reel count not be added to make a total. The recommendation that microfilm be counted in reels is consistent with the physical volume of printed materials.

Microcard and microfiche, which tend to be bought in series, are best reported by the piece, since one serial subscription may cover thousands of cards.

For each of the above categories, list the number added during the year and the number withdrawn during the year.

6 *List special collections of library materials not included above only if warranted by depth or amount; count by individual item.*

For national statistics, it is not recommended that a further breakdown in reporting be made. However, further breakdown of categories of library holdings may be made for internal administrative use, and to facilitate comparisons between libraries that wish to do so. A standard method of counting should be adopted by all libraries even for those materials which are not now reported nationally in the event that these items become of national significance at some future time.

Methods for counting nonbook materials are here outlined in order to make them uniform. Count by the piece: broadsides, posters, manuscripts, sheet maps (if bound, include in volume count), pictures, prints, photographs, and unbound sheet music. Prints, maps, or plates in portfolio are counted as volumes. Audiovisual materials should also be counted individually. Slides and filmstrips should be counted by the piece. Motion picture film is counted by the reel. Sound recordings on disc, spool of wire, or reel of tape are counted by the physical unit.

Telephone books, college and trade catalogs, etc., are ephemera and should not be reported. Other material which does not fall into the recommended format for national reporting, but which is of significance due to amount or depth, should be listed by libraries individually.

7 *Omit office book-collections and other collections on campus not part of library.*

Special material available on campus but not administered by the library should not be counted in the library collection. This includes office book-collections and audio-visual materials which are located on campus but not part of the library holdings.

8 *Count government documents by item; do not add to the total volume count. Add periodical subscriptions as in recommendation 3. Determine if library is a U.S. Government document depository.*

Count government documents by item when they do not fit the volume definition; they should be reported separately from the total volume count. In this context, the Superintendent of Government classification system is not interpreted as "classified" according to the definition of a volume. Pamphlets, press releases, or other unbound materials should not be prorated into volumes. A government publication should be added to the volume count when it is hardbound or paperbound and locally classified.

Since most government documents are published serially, only periodical titles so identified in the February issue of the *U.S. Government Publications Monthly Catalog* should be counted under current subscriptions.

The question of whether or not a library is a U.S. Government document depository should be included in order to assist the user in the interpretation of the data for the library.

Circulation

RECOMMENDATION

Omit for national reporting

Insofar as circulation figures represent library use, they fall short of their intent. Coupled with attendance figures, or room count, they may be somewhat more significant. While it may be worthwhile for a library's internal operation to know peak periods and relative use of various service stations, it is not believed possible to derive nationally comparable data, owing to variation in loan periods, in "reserve" policies, and in centralized or decentralized operations. It is recommended that circulation statistics for college and university libraries not be reported nationally.

If circulation figures are needed for analytical purposes within a library, they will be useful in their own terms. Short-term loans, reserves, faculty loan periods, or renewals may be compared among libraries within the same system. Coupled with information on whether a library has open or closed stacks or a combination of both, the hours the library is open, and the number of hours during which charge-out stations are serviced, circulation figures will be useful in a special study of library use.

Photoduplication

RECOMMENDATION

Omit for national reporting

There has been some consideration of photoduplication as a measurable part of the library's circulation function. As a standard measure, this function is so fractionalized as to make any substantive statement in relation to it illusory. If the number of microfilms made were counted, it would have to be subdivided by reels made for academic departments and reels to be added to the library's collection. Reels to be added to the library's collection will be counted by acquisition, regardless of where they were made. Even if a double count were made here, a report of the number of reels of microfilm made does not give an indication of circulation figures. Further, the number of articles and parts of books, charts, maps, and students' notes reproduced would have to be counted as sheets. Both methods of counting would have to exclude work done for and counted by interlibrary loan. Since none of this material is returned to the library, it is not a valid measure of circulation.

Interlibrary Loan Transactions

RECOMMENDATIONS

1 *Count items borrowed and items lent.*
2 *Omit unfilled requests received.*
3 *Omit breakdown by kind, etc.*
4 *Omit intralibrary loans.*

Interlibrary loan transactions supplement the reference function of a library and supplant, to some extent, its circulation function. The dynamics of library service are linked with changing demands. The number of interlibrary loans made among institutions reflects the interdependence between even the largest institutions. The figures reported may be due to agreements between institutions to purchase in depth in assigned areas, or they may reflect basic weaknesses in collections. In some research libraries, a restricted circulation policy and a strong subject specialization tend to increase interlibrary loan activities.

The mode of filling a request, that is, by sending the material itself, or by sending a photocopy, should not affect the count. Unfilled requests should not be counted. As an aid to qualitative assessment of use of a library, it would occasionally be helpful to make a subject breakdown of material requested as a special study. Both the academic department requesting material, and the subject classification of the material requested, would give an indication of gaps in the library collection.

Count completed transactions by physical volume, reel, or microcard by the piece, and unbounds by the piece. Omit intralibrary loans, that is, those made within the system.

Reference Service

National data are not feasible at this time.

Services rendered by the reference departments of college and university libraries consist of much more than answering informational questions. Such services include building and keeping the reference collection up to date and compiling bibliographies. Until the main variables (such as time, education and training of the reference librarian, quality of available reference tools, and heterogeneity and level of clientele) are measured and combined into an index, reference service can be measured only in crude terms.

Reference questions, as such, can be measured in terms of number of contacts, time consumed per question, or number of questions handled. The number of contacts or people asking questions does not reveal the number of questions asked. Time spent may be dependent upon the resources of the library and their accessibility, and upon the resources of the librarian and his familiarity with the subject and the collection. While all of these are valid criteria, none individually provides a true picture.

Personnel

The number of positions by type in college and university libraries, and the salaries paid in each class, are of general interest and usefulness. The uses of personnel statistics are of internal as well as national import. Management analysis, methods studies and work flow charting, the ratio of librarian positions to other professional and nonprofessional positions, and studies of salary *vs.* other expenditures depend on clear definitions and precise terminology. Comparison with practices in other institutions will reveal trends in staffing, and comparison of vacancies with the number of library school graduates will delineate the professional market place.

It is recommended that personnel data be reported not at the end of a fiscal year but on a date which is presumed to occur during a stable period. November 1 is suggested as an optimum date.

RECOMMENDATIONS

1 *Report total number of filled positions on staff by type, in full time equivalents (FTE).*

2 *Report number of vacancies, by position classification.*

3 *Report number of incumbents who have fifth-year library school degrees.*

4 *Report number of full-time librarians and other professionals, by position classification and salary bracket.*

Determination of the number of library staff positions requires a count of three elements: full-time positions, part-time positions, and vacant positions. A full-time position is one that requires the incumbent to work the total work week of the library. Full-time equivalents of part-time positions should be determined by adding all the hours worked per week in all part-time positions within the desired category, and dividing it by the number of hours within the total work week of the library. When fractional positions result, any fraction up to one-half should be dropped, and any fraction one-half or over should be rounded to the next whole number.

To improve comparability in reporting among libraries, it is recommended that these data be requested in terms of positions rather than in terms of the incumbents of these positions. A position can be classified into one of the three areas with less bias than would exist if the qualifications of the incumbent of the position were considered.

The positions of maintenance and operational personnel should be excluded; they are not significant in the evaluation of the library program, and they are usually not included with the library staff roster.

Number of Filled and Vacant Positions

| | Professional | | |
Item	Librarians	Other	Nonprofessional
Number of full-time positions filled			
Number of part-time positions filled (in full-time equivalents)			
Total filled positions (in full-time equivalents)			
Number of vacant positions			

Since the amount of academic training is not specifically indicated in the definition as a requisite for a professional position, the following question should be included:

How many library school graduates holding a fifth-year degree in librarianship are on the staff?_____

Statistics which fully describe characteristics of library staff members would have to be the subject of a special study.

> 5 *Report salaries separately for staff members employed 9-10 months and 11-12 months. If services are contributed, report a salary equivalent for 11-12 month employment.*

Because library staff salaries are usually confidential, it is not practical to ask for the specific salary paid to each staff member.

Suggested Reporting Form

Salaries of Full-Time Professional Staff Members

currently employed

Position	Total	Less than $4,000	$4,000 to $4,999	(etc. by $1,000 steps to)	$19,000 to $19,999	$20,000 or more
Chief Librarian						
Deputy, associate, or assistant librarians						
Department/Division Heads						
Heads of school and college libraries within universities						
All other librarians and professionals						
Total						

NOTE.—This table should be presented in three parts: (*a*) 9-10 months, (*b*) 11-12 months, and (*c*) contributed services.

The salary brackets in the table are detailed enough to provide useful salary distributions and averages for homogeneous groups. Reporting should be based on the actual contract salary paid, before any deductions. For full-time professional staff members within a particular position classification, the number receiving salaries which fall in a given bracket should be reported in that cell of the table.

Since salary data are more useful when current, it is recommended that salary data be reported as of the academic year in which the survey is being conducted rather than for the previous academic year.

In order to improve the homogeneity of the reported salary data, the current practice of indicating term of employment in 9-10 month or 11-12 month periods should be continued. In addition, contributed services, which constitute the monetary value of library work performed by denominational groups (including members of religious orders), should be equated with 11-12 month salaries paid to lay staff in the institution and reported separately.

Physical Facilities

RECOMMENDATIONS

1 *Report central library, branch and departmental libraries, and extension center libraries as part of library system.*

2 *Report autonomous libraries on same campus separately, but add to total of campus.*

3 *Report libraries on other campuses separately.*

Number of Units. Physical facilities for college and university libraries should be reported in terms of the main library, the number of branches in buildings which are physically separate from the main library, and libraries on other campuses. The number of branches should include extension center libraries, administratively autonomous libraries located on campus (such as law or medical libraries), and libraries on the same campus but supported by independent endowment funds. Total statistics reported should include all of the above with the exception of libraries on other campuses. These should be reported separately, but it is recommended that statistics be coordinated by and reported through the main campus library.

4 *Report area in gross square footage.*

5 *Report seating capacity according to chairs available in a defined area. (Include carrels, lounge chairs, conference rooms, and seminar rooms, but exclude classrooms and auditoriums.)*

6 *Report volume capacity in a single total for open stack, closed stack, and storage area (stack or compact).*

Capacity Measurements. It is recommended that the reporting of area measurements for college and university libraries be in terms of gross square footage (see glossary). Although nonlibrary functional areas are included in this total, the ratio of library to nonlibrary use-areas is relatively constant. Converting from one to the other would not be difficult. Gross square footage has been recommended both because of the ease with which this measure can be obtained and the fact that library building-cost ratios are usually expressed in terms of gross square feet.[8]

For statistical reporting, it is recommended that seating capacity (see glossary) be requested. In addition, a question on volume capacity (see glossary) should be included.

Detailed information concerning specific library areas, such as reader area, work area, stack area, etc., may be obtained by special study.

Operating Expenditures

RECOMMENDATIONS

1 *List operating expenditures for personnel, library materials, binding, and other operating expenditures, and total.*

2 *Include initial outlay for books and library materials under "Expenditures for Library Materials," but indicate by footnote.*

3 *Omit total capital expenditures.*

4 *Omit utility services.*

It is recommended that only actual expenditures, as opposed to allocations, be reported. Expenditures are usually divided into two broad categories, operating expenditures and capital expenditures. Only those items which are deemed of significance in budget preparation and justification are included in national

---

[8]Construction-cost data can be converted from one region to another by using indices such as those published monthly in *Architectural Record,* and other F. W. Dodge construction-cost statistics. There is also a government index published which gives building-cost indices by region.

reporting. The separate categories are described below. Monies expended for books and other library materials should be reported under operating expenditures; when the expenditure represents an initial outlay for stock in a new library, it should be indicated by a footnote.

Expenditures for personnel
> Include salaries and wages before any deductions. Social security, retirement, pension contributions, and other "fringe benefits" paid by the institution should not be included in operating expenditures. (These items are normally included as part of the institution's over-all expenditure report.) For libraries operating their own binderies, exclude salaries and wages for that operation.

Expenditures for library materials
> Include book stock, periodicals and serials, microform, audio-visual and other nonbook materials. Initial outlay expenditures to be indicated by footnote.

Expenditures for binding
> For libraries operating their own binderies, report total expenditure figures, including those for salaries, wages, and supplies.

Other operating expenditures
> Include expenditures for building operation and maintenance, and other expenditures such as supplies, stationery, printing, postage and freight, travel, memberships, replacement of equipment and furnishings, and insurance. Exclude expenditures for utilities.

Total operating expenditures

Capital Expenditures

Include building sites, new buildings and additions, renovation, equipment for new or expanded buildings, audio-visual equipment, microform equipment, and investment properties.

NOTE.—It is not required that capital expenditures be collected or published annually.

III

Statistics of

Public Libraries

Definition

Public library agencies in the United States present a multi-faceted and often contradictory picture. Any attempt to coordinate statistics among them and to bring large areas of public library service into focus must first deal squarely with the question as to which agencies should be included. The definition of a public library must be broad enough to allow for differences in government, source of income, service area, and nature of collection; but there is also a point at which an agency ceases to be a public library.

To be included in public library statistics, every agency must offer *free* services to everyone within some stipulated geographical area. Libraries which do *not*, whether from tradition as old subscription or corporation libraries or from extreme financial pressure, should not be considered public and should not be included.

The point at which a collection of books available to the public ceases to be a valid unit for national statistical purposes is determined arbitrarily. It is suggested that unless the agency is a member of a library system, it must meet *all of the following criteria* to be included in public library statistics:

1 Give at least 10 hours of public service per week
2 Have a book collection of at least 2,000 volumes
3 Purchase at least 200 volumes per year
4 Expend at least $1,000 per year

These criteria are not intended to relate to, or to set minimum standards of, library service. They merely indicate the lowest level at which an agency can be considered a statistical unit. Inclusion of figures for libraries which do not meet all of these criteria negates the concepts of "population served" and "area served," and distorts all total figures of public library resources and services. School-public library combinations present particular statistical problems. Because data on these two functions often cannot be separated accurately, it is recommended that such libraries be included wholly in either school library statistics or public library statistics, as follows:

If the library is located in a school, is administered by a person certified under state certification requirements for teachers, and is open during school hours, it should be counted as a school library. Public library services and extended hours are incidental to its primary purpose as a school library.

If the library is physically located in a school but is established under public library laws, and serves only incidentally the library needs of teachers and pupils because there is no school library, then it will be counted as a public library.

Organization

Public library statistics should be so tabulated as to bring similar agencies together for comparison. To do so requires basic classification by some critical characteristic, such as type of government, source of funds, area or population served, size of collection, or size of budget. Which classification is used depends upon the purpose to which the statistics are put. Once the particular classification has been decided upon, it may be necessary to design two or more questionnaires according to the size or complexity of the units being studied.

There is a question, however, as to what constitutes the library unit being tabulated. Should a library which is a member of a library system be reported separately or within total figures for that system? Should the figures for the central library of a large city be lost within total figures including branches, deposit stations, bookmobiles, etc.? Likewise, should the separate identity of all the cooperating or affiliated units of rural library systems be lost in the whole?

All units within a system, whether consolidated or loosely federated, constitute service outlets sharing staff and book resources among them according to some plan. It may be desirable at certain times, and for special purposes, to obtain detailed data regarding each service outlet; but such a level of detail is beyond the scope of national reporting and the present coordination effort. The nature of the statistical coverage would have to be predicated on the purpose and scope of the special study.

Of more concern is the fact that the range and depth of library services available to the public cannot be revealed through statistics of any one system outlet, with the possible exception of the central headquarters unit. The number of books at one of the smaller outlets loses meaning as intrasystem loans, deposit collections, and central reference services are developed. Similarly, the amount of local expenditures by a member library does little to reflect the true volume and scope of services available through the close relationship with the system center and the dependence upon pooled resources.

One of the axioms which underlie the system concept is that *the whole is greater than the sum of its parts.* At the same time, the total of the book collections of a number of smaller libraries does not represent the same strength (i.e., breadth and depth of resources) as a similar number of books held by one library, since there is an inevitable and desirable duplication of titles. The size of the central core, or headquarters collection, has a great deal to do with the quality of the system resources and is the factor which makes the above axiom possible.

Statistics for library systems should show two aspects:

1 Total figures for all libraries, branches, and service outlets within the system.
2 Separate statistics for the system center (i.e., headquarters library only, excluding branches, deposit stations, bookmobiles, and affiliated libraries).

At this point we again meet the problems which the enormous diversity of public libraries and library systems presents. We need only scan developments in the last ten years to realize that the system concept is still very young. Library systems at this stage of their development, therefore, present an inevitable lack of uniformity. When we try to apply the two statistical approaches above, what happens where there is no system center (i.e., basic book and staff services reservoir); where, for example, several "regional" libraries are being coordinated by a purely administrative headquarters? In such a case, no separate figures can be given for the system center, and the statistics should be footnoted accordingly to reveal this important fact. The same can be said of the system where each unit specializes in certain subject areas for eventual use by all units.

A system center sometimes delegates central functions (or resources) to system outlets. When these functions can be identified and measured, they should be included in the figures for the system center. An example of this would be a city library system's business branch whose resources are not duplicated at the central library. This collection should be included in the central library statistics, rather than with other service outlets.

The following discussion of public library statistics does not include per capita measurements, unit costs, and other derived statistics. Also, the questions within each category are far from exhaustive. They are intended as a uniform starting point from which further studies in depth can be made. To cover all of the areas of public library operations in which questions might be asked would be impossible. At the same time, basic understanding and agreement as to primary statistical factors and standard definitions are essential for further studies.

Identification

Many of the questions asked of libraries for the purpose of identifying them are more essential to a directory of library agencies than to statistical reporting. Quite often both functions are fulfilled with one survey, and this overlapping of function can be seen in the illustrative items below.

Of prime statistical importance is identification of the year for which the figures are supplied. Because fiscal years of public libraries are far from uniform, one method of clarifying the reporting period is to include those reports of completed fiscal years in which a given January falls.

Identification of the municipality in which the library is located is necessary to the determination of service area, as will be seen in the discussion under "Area Served," p.35. Items of identification should include the following:

1 Fiscal year ending _____

2 Name of library _____

3 Mailing address _____

4 Location of library (i.e., central library or administrative headquarters):

Municipality in which located_____

County _____

State _____

5 Name of Head Librarian_____

Government

Most public libraries are governed in one of two ways. Either the agency is a branch of local government, with the librarian reporting directly to the local government authorities, or it is governed by a library board. Such a board may or may not be a creation of the local government. The following items are designed to reveal the basic relationships among the library, its source of funds, and the service area for which it has primary responsibility:

1 Head Librarian is directly responsible to: (check)

_____ local government official(s) or unit (e.g., mayor, city manager, county commissioner, board of education, etc.)

_____ Library Board

2 If Head Librarian reports to local government, give title of the official to whom he reports _____

3 If Head Librarian is responsible to the Library Board, give the number of board members appointed or elected by:

_____ city or town _____ community groups or organizations

_____ township

_____ county _____ library association

_____ school district _____ library board (self-perpetuating)

_____ other (specify)

Population of Service Area

Public libraries face the question of "population served" from many different angles. By definition, they must provide their full services free of charge at the request of anyone living within a given geographical area, usually that from which tax support derives. In addition, however, there may be certain groups or individuals living outside that area to whom library privileges are also extended—school children from a neighboring community or families of persons who are employed in the area but reside elsewhere.

Technically, "population served" is the number of persons who have access to the library. Although many people do not use a library, the number who *can* use it is the preferred statistic, and should be measured in terms of U.S. Census figures for local governmental units. The Census *population of the service area* is the only measurable and reliable figure. A count of those persons who have actually availed themselves of the library's services cannot be used for several reasons:

A count of registered borrowers will not measure the number of persons who come into the library for on-the-spot use, nor will it show the number of people who use the same card (friends or members of the same family).

Attendance, or door-counts of people entering the building, are unmanageable for most small and medium-sized public libraries. It would not be feasible to separate the cardholders from the non-cardholders in an attendance count. Thus, using this kind of figure to supplement that of registered borrowers would result in double counting of persons served.

Library service to community groups and service through mass communication media involve a clientele which cannot be counted, and would also result in double counting of persons served.

The U.S. Census figures for the service area are not only a convenient solution to the question of "population served," they also relate library statistics to those which reveal characteristics of the community. Educational and economic levels, factors regarding national origin, religion, race, etc., bear upon the resources and services which the library must strive to develop. For library statistics to be used in conjunction with such information, the U.S. Census base for population of the service area is essential. When special studies of a particular region are conducted between decennial censuses, the use of authoritative population estimates may be warranted. If use of official state estimates is mandatory to understand certain data, such figures should be listed in addition to the U.S. census figures. Since state estimates are made at varying times and employ varying methodology, the U.S. Census figures remain the only consistent, comparable population base for multistate and national reporting.

Area Served

Having agreed that U.S. Census figures are to be used to determine the population figures, the question of area served necessarily becomes a matter of how many governmental units are involved. It is at this point that problems of overlapping service areas must be faced, because two or more libraries may claim service to the same governmental unit.

It is recommended that the state's questionnaire require each public library to identify the governmental units which contribute to local library support. From these reports, however, the state must screen out overlapping service areas and adjust figures for total population served before submitting them for national tabulations.

Certain problems are raised by confining "area served" to those governmental units contributing tax funds[1] for library support. First, what about public libraries which receive no tax funds? Are libraries which are established as memorials, for example, and which may be generously endowed, not to be statistically measured? Can one assume that absence of tax income means absence of library service? How does one define the area served if the area buying the service cannot be identified?

A compromise, or more properly an allowance for exception, must be reached. Libraries not receiving tax funds would be included in statistical reports if they met all of the four minimum criteria outlined previously (see page 30). Area and population served would be reported as only that of the municipality in which the library is located. Questions regarding population and area served can be posed in the following manner:

> List the governmental units which contribute tax funds to the library (whether by direct tax, appropriation, or contract), along with the latest U.S. Census population figures for each.
> List any additional governmental units which do not contribute tax funds, but to which the library offers all of its services free of charge. (Areas receiving only partial service should not be included, because the variables entailed would work against comparability among libraries.)
> If the library does not receive tax funds, report the municipality in which it is located.

If service areas are measured in terms of school districts and the only population figures available do not coincide with the U.S. Census figures for local governmental units, this fact should be revealed by means of a footnote.

---

[1] "Tax funds" is used rather than "public funds" so as to distinguish such income from contributions and fund drives. The latter income would be considered "gifts."

Registration

It is recommended that comparative statistics for registration not be collected because they bear little relation to library use and lack uniformity. For example:

The extent and frequency of library use by cardholders is not shown. One may have used the library once; another may be borrowing regularly for a whole family.

The length of registration not only varies from library to library but may even be indefinite.

Some libraries do not remove from the registration files those obsolete cards resulting from change of address, death, etc.

Registration shows neither on-the-spot use of the library nor the number of persons served through interlibrary loan.

Because registration files provide valuable data for research into characteristics of library users, it would be helpful to know of their existence. It is recommended that the following question be included:

Do you maintain registration files? _____Yes _____No

Physical Facilities; Agencies of Service; Hours Open

Data concerning physical facilities are needed occasionally to assess adequacy of book capacity, seating capacity, working conditions, and other factors. Current legislation directed toward library construction will also call for basic information on library buildings, both for planning and evaluation. Since physical facilities do not change rapidly, there is less need for updating statistics. Questions regarding library buildings need not be asked annually.

As a special study, or perhaps once every five years, facts should be gathered regarding the following:

Whether the library is in a separate building
Date of erection of building housing central library
Year of last major improvement or addition to building
Square feet of floor space
Volume capacity of central library
Seating capacity in reading rooms

Because data regarding cost of the library building are difficult to supply for library facilities housed within other buildings (e.g., schools, municipal buildings, community centers) and because cost figures for replacement of buildings involve complex adjustment factors for comparability, cost data should be gathered only as a special study.

In judging the amount and type of service the library offers its public and the extent to which it attempts to maximize access, it is important to have data regarding the number of service outlets maintained. The following information on service outlets administered by the central library should be requested annually:

Total number of branches (see glossary)
Total number of deposit stations (see glossary) excluding classroom collections in schools
Total number of classroom collections in schools
Number of bookmobiles (excluding delivery vehicles from which public service is not given)

To ascertain the size and nature of a library system, include the following item concerning other system outlets (i.e., affiliated libraries or member libraries not administered by the central library):

If the library serves as a system headquarters, give number of cooperating public libraries (members of system).

The number of hours open per week is asked of the central library only and is asked in terms of the library's predominant schedule. While hours of service could be computed on an annual basis and thus help resolve problems of shifting summer and winter schedules, holidays, and weekends, such a figure is awkward. People think in terms of weekly schedules, whether they be laymen reading the statistical report or librarians trying to supply the data. Questions regarding evening and weekend hours are included because they are specifically mentioned in national standards and show the extent to which the library attempts to serve all of the residents in its community.

Total number of hours open per week
for public service (predominant schedule) _____
Number of evening hours (after 6:00 P.M.)
per week _____
Number of hours open on Saturday _____
Number of hours open on Sunday _____

Library Collection (Resources)

There are two main purposes to which statistics concerning library resources are usually put—determination of building-space needs and evaluation of the scope of the collection. Of these, the first is essentially a matter of concern to the individual library; the second, however, is vital to comparison of libraries and evaluation of library services. Insofar as possible, a library should maintain an accurate count of those items which are its stock in trade. A current study[2] points out that reported figures often differ drastically from actual counts. While it is recognized that a complete library inventory is often not possible because of the time and expense involved, an effort should be made to obtain a simple count of the library's resources and to maintain accurate records as to additions and withdrawals.

As indicated in the introduction to this chapter, figures should be supplied for the system as a whole, as well as for the headquarters collection separately.

Book stock should be counted in volumes, meaning physical units; government documents are to be counted by the piece; periodicals are counted by titles and bibliographic volumes; nonbook materials are counted by the physical item. Since the unit count differs from category to category, a count within each category of the items in microform is not required. (However, where microform can be counted by the unit called for, it should be included. For example, the number of titles and bibliographic volumes comprising the periodicals collection should include microform as well as full-size material.)

Generally, microform is most conveniently counted in terms of physical units, i.e., number of reels, microcards, and microfiches. To superimpose this count on each of the four categories would be impractical for annual reporting. It is suggested that detailed information regarding holdings in microform be the subject of a special study.

Book Stock. Book stock (counted in volumes) should include the information called for in the following table. Adult book stock has not been divided into fiction and nonfiction, for the following reasons:

Other statistics to which it could be related cannot readily be collected in this fashion (circulation).

Other factors would influence the evaluation of these data (size of library).

---

[2]Kenneth E. Beasley, *Statistical Reporting System for Local Public Libraries* (University Park: Pennsylvania State University, Institute of Public Administration, 1964).

Unless it can be related to other items that are being collected, it is not considered important to the national statistics program.

Most libraries have already given up trying to differentiate between juvenile fiction and nonfiction.

Book Stock

	Adult Book Stock	Juvenile Book Stock	TOTAL
No. volumes at beginning of year			
No. volumes added* during year			
No. volumes lost or withdrawn during year			
No. volumes at end of year			

*An item is considered added when it is recorded in the public catalog and made available for use. Detail as to how added (by purchase, gift or exchange) is considered unnecessary for national reporting.

In addition to counting volumes, it would be highly desirable for libraries to report the number of titles which are individually cataloged (i.e., for which there are main entries in the catalog). While most libraries cannot at present supply information as to number of titles at beginning of year, they should begin to keep records as to number of titles added and withdrawn. Eventually, as library systems develop, data on number of titles should be kept in the same manner as number of volumes. Libraries and systems can then be more accurately compared in terms of the amount of information they contain.

The following question should be added to those above:

Number of new titles added during year _____

Government Documents. Government documents often constitute a separate collection of library materials. When this is the case, the total number of physical items at the end of the year should be reported separately; otherwise they will inflate total figures and impair comparability of library collections. Such counts preferably should not include material which is to be superseded by permanent cumulative volumes. Documents which are fully cataloged and intershelved with books will be counted as "Book Stock"; periodicals which bear a government imprint but are treated as part of the periodicals collection would be counted with other periodicals; documents held in vertical files with other ephemera would be counted with non-book materials.

If the library is a documents depository, this fact should be revealed through the following questions:

Is the library designated a documents depository by the federal government?

If so, in what year was it so designated?

Is the library designated a documents depository by the state government?

If so, in what year was it designated?

Periodicals Collection. Periodicals collection is meant to include periodicals, newspapers, and any other serials not included

---

Periodicals Collection

	Number of Titles Currently Received*	Number of Bibliographic Volumes Held
Periodicals (excluding newspapers and other serials)		
Newspapers		
Other serials (not included in Book Stock)		
Totals		

*Again, the manner in which these items are acquired (by purchase, gift, or exchange) would be a detail for special study only.

---

under book stock or nonbook materials. In the case of periodicals collection, the number of titles is even more important than with book stock, and statistics should be provided to afford comparison between the number of titles currently received and the number of volumes. In this way, some indication can be given as to the number of back issues available.

It is recommended that "volumes" of periodicals refer to *bibliographic volumes,* i.e., the unit established by the publisher as a volume. Binding practices vary so greatly that the number of physical units held distorts comparability of collections of periodicals. Bibliographic volumes may be cited whether the material is bound, unbound, or on microfilm or microcards. Although it is recognized that the form in which this material is kept affects public access to it, and therefore its use, it is not considered necessary to identify the number of titles on microfilm or the number of reels on a recurring national basis. The "Periodicals Collection" table illustrates information to be elicited.

A library retains back issues indefinitely or discards on a regular or irregular basis (e.g., back issues discarded after five years). The following items should be included which would reveal the library's policy with regard to discarding:

Indicate the number of periodicals titles retained in back files for the following periods:
Number of titles kept up to and including 5 years _____
Number of titles kept over 5 years but not indefinitely
_____
Number of titles kept indefinitely _____

Library systems should report for both the system as a whole and the headquarters collection separately.

Nonbook Materials. Into this last category of library resources falls a vast multitude of materials, in some instances varying from filmstrips to sheet music. An enumeration of possible nonbook materials would be out of the question. Still, the statistical questionnaire should cite enough examples to assist the librarian in reporting all of the various other resources the library may offer its clientele. The questionnaire should also be explicit enough to guide the respondent around the pitfalls of double-counting and confusion with items to be reported under book stock and periodicals collection.

A problem which becomes evident in statistical reporting of nonbook materials is that of the relative value the library places

Nonbook Materials

	Total at Beginning of Year	Number Added	Number Withdrawn	Total at End of Year
Audio-Visual Materials*				
Films				
Filmstrips				
Slides				
Recordings (discs and tapes)				
Other				
Materials for the blind†				
Talking books (discs and tapes)				
Braille materials				
Other				
Other Itemized Nonbook Materials				
Pamphlets				
Catalogs (college and trade)				
Manuscripts				
Sheet music				
Maps				
Pictures, photographs				
Framed pictures				
Other (specify)				

*Counted by physical item (reel, strip, slide, disc, or tape).
†Materials for the blind or otherwise visually handicapped people should be reported separately from other audio-visual materials. It is recommended, however, that questionnaires not include this category each year.

upon them. A large public library will tend to maintain records on almost all of its materials. It will be able to report figures for the number of nonbook materials at the beginning of the year, the number added, the number withdrawn, and the total number at the end of the year. A small library, however, might find such records burdensome, impractical, and unnecessary. Where counts by item are maintained, figures should be reported; but recurring statistics should not require detailed record keeping of all nonbook materials.

Two factors influence whether a particular library resource is counted with book stock or with nonbook materials. There is the obvious factor of form, but there is also the factor mentioned before—the relative importance which the library places upon the material. Pamphlets, technical reports, and many other printed items which do not meet the definition of a "book" can be counted in either category. The determining factor is whether or not the item is represented in the catalog. If it is, it should be counted with book stock; if not, with nonbook materials.

Item counts should be available for audio-visual materials and often for some other categories of nonbook materials. The latter would have to be specified by the individual library. When nonbook materials are itemized, the number of items should be provided according to the table.

Nonbook materials which are not itemized are often a mixture of various physical forms interfiled in vertical files, pamphlet boxes, and shelf files (e.g., pamphlets, leaflets, pictures, clippings, etc.) and are not itemized. The volume of such nonbook materials should be indicated in linear feet of materials filed. If materials are in vertical files, only that portion of the file drawer which is filled should be reported. Such reporting, as against number of file drawers, will bring the figures into comparability with shelf files, and will get around the problem of partially filled drawers. The question could be worded as follows:

Nonbook materials not itemized   *Number of linear feet*
    (in vertical files, pamphlet boxes,
    shelf files, etc.) ....   _____

Total Library Holdings. It is recommended that *no figure* be given which would attempt to add together, in one grand total, the subtotals of book stock, periodicals collection, and nonbook materials. To do so would be to combine totally unlike units and produce a figure which cannot be used to compare libraries. Such a catch-all figure might have dubious merit as a status symbol, but it has no validity as a library statistic.

Circulation

Many arguments are leveled against circulation statistics, not the least of which is that they can be readily manipulated by the individual library with a subsequent loss of comparability among libraries. Factors such as length of loan period and renewal policy affect circulation totals, sometimes drastically. Criticism is also made with respect to overemphasis of these data. It is generally understood by librarians that circulation figures give

Direct Circulation Service

	Adult Circulation	Juvenile Circulation	Total
Central library			
All other service outlets			
Total			

an imperfect and incomplete picture of library use. It is also probable that these figures have been subjected to abuse, since many laymen look upon them as a principal indication of the volume of business. At the same time, trends in circulation are important. If a standard method of counting can be agreed upon, circulation figures undoubtedly will help to describe in part the library's activity and clientele, at least relatively.

The total number of materials circulated should be reported by the place from which the materials are charged out (central library, system outlets), and by the manner of loan (direct loan, interlibrary loan). Provisions of photocopies in lieu of circulation should also be shown, but photocopying for other purposes, such as acquisition of material for the library's collection, should be screened out of such figures.

It is increasingly difficult to count circulation by type of material because of the use of automatic charging systems in place of book cards. In many cases the library will not be able to tell from the transaction record whether the item circulated was an item of book stock, an item from its periodicals collection, or an item from its audio-visual materials or other nonbook materials. Adult materials can usually be distinguished from juvenile materials, but fiction may not be distinguished from nonfiction. Most detailed data regarding circulation by type of material must be gathered by special studies and spot checks.

The table illustrates points which are of significance for public libraries. It is recommended, however, that with regard to national reporting, consideration be given to the use of "trend" figures rather than these gross numbers. It would be more significant to know whether the library's circulation had increased or decreased since the last reporting period than to be able to compare its circulation figure with that of another agency. A "percentage change" figure would also eliminate the errors due to differing loan periods, charging systems, and methods of record keeping. They could be internally consistent even though derived from different bases.

In addition, total figures should be supplied for the following:

Interlibrary loan service:
    Number of interlibrary loans filled
    Number of interlibrary loans obtained
Photocopy service:
    Number of photocopies supplied in lieu of circulation
Number of items sent to schools for circulation from classroom
    collections

Although interlibrary loan has been placed within the area of circulation in order to be counted among total items charged out, there may be need to transfer this part of the table elsewhere for statistical clarity and convenience. Libraries often find it profitable also to record the number of interlibrary loans requested but not filled. This is a statistic more necessary for the individual library, however. Coordination of these figures with those of other libraries is not a recognized need.

The question arises as to whether the circulation of an item to a patron should be counted twice under interlibrary loan—once at the library actually owning the item and again at the library which has obtained it through interlibrary loan. From the standpoint of the circulation function, this double-counting is required and inevitable. The effort to obtain the material and thus perform a service is just as valid whether the material is obtained from the collection, from another library, or from a dealer by purchase.

Problems of counting photocopies supplied in lieu of circulation of materials must be considered. The number of pages supplied is dependent upon the type of copier used so that this figure has little meaning. A reproduction of a book or a part of a book should be counted as a single item. Photocopy reproductions prepared from periodical material, however, should be counted in terms of the number of articles copied, a full article or part of an article being counted as a single item.

One problem deserves special attention: that of reporting cir-

culation of classroom collections at schools. At present, counting
methods include the following:

One circulation per deposit book per month (Boston)
Classroom collections counted three per deposit book; other
   collections, one per deposit book (Baltimore)
Two circulations per book per month (Cincinnati)
Four circulations per semester for each book (Milwaukee)

It is recommended that libraries not multiply the number of
books on deposit by the number of pupils in the class. To do so
inflates circulation figures and impedes valid comparison with
other libraries. Unless figures of actual use can be obtained, classroom circulation should be counted only once per item—at the
time the item leaves the public library. To use the other methods
would be misleading.

Reference Services

It has long been agreed that reference statistics are needed
(1) to justify funds expended for these services, (2) to evaluate
reference performance and resources, and (3) to measure work
load. Despite considerable inquiry in the past plus continuing
interest and efforts in this area, the profession has not come to
any agreement that present methods of counting can either apply
to a significant number of libraries or differentiate succinctly the
varying levels of service rendered.

At present, the problem of measuring reference service is approached from three viewpoints:

1 Number and type of inquiries:
   Tabulation as to reference questions answered and unan-
      swered; categorization into levels of difficulty (e.g., "quick
      information," "search," "research"; or requiring less than
      one hour, over one hour); identification of the manner in
      which the question was received (in person, by tele-
      phone, by mail); simple total of reference transactions
2 Record of sources used:
   Number of books reshelved; number of sources consulted by
      reference assistants; categorization of reference sources
      consulted by broad subject area
3 Count of clientele:
   Regular or occasional counts of readers entering the refer-
      ence department or coming to the reference desk; spot
      checks on number of readers at particular times of day

All of these methods and various combinations of them have been used, but rarely has confidence been placed in the accuracy of the resulting figures. That any one of them can be applied by all types and sizes of public libraries is highly doubtful; that the statistics so gathered are truly meaningful to the public or even to the profession can be questioned.

The reporting of the number of reference transactions (excluding internal directional questions) is recommended as a recurring statistic, but only as an indication of the size of the operation. Additional special study of the problem must take place before any attempt is made to coordinate findings.

Technical Services

Almost all of the figures which can be reported under cataloging, classification, acquisitions, binding, and other areas of technical services of a library are primarily work-load figures used for purposes of internal control. Statistical coordination in this area, therefore, is primarily a matter of uniform definitions; no questions regarding details or amounts of technical processes are recommended here other than those which are inherent within the concepts pertaining to the growth of the collection. The source of data regarding volumes and titles is obviously within the technical services area. Such data, however, are concerned with enumeration of the finished products which constitute the library's holdings rather than the number of activities which have gone into preparation of the material for use by the clientele. Data regarding numbers of volumes and titles are requested in "Library Collection," p.38.

Cost and budget figures relating to technical services will be discussed in "Expenditures," p.54.

It is recognized, however, that reliable data on the basic trends in technical services may prove to be of long-term significance. As a special study, it is recommended that public libraries be asked questions on the activity of the library in the purchase of catalog cards and precataloged books, the operation of its own bindery, and the use of a published classification system.

Personnel

The number of positions in public libraries and the salaries paid in each class are of general interest and usefulness. It is proposed that questions be asked in the following categories in order to obtain needed statistics.

Number of Library Staff Positions. The determination of the number of library staff positions requires a count of three elements: full-time filled positions, part-time filled positions, and vacant positions. A full-time position is one that requires the incumbent to work at least thirty-five hours per week or the total work week of the library, whichever is greater. Full-time equivalency of part-time positions should be determined by adding all the hours worked per week in all part-time positions within the desired category and dividing it by the number of hours within the total work week of the library. When fractional positions result, any fraction up to one-half should be dropped, and any fraction one-half or over should be rounded to the next full number.

The statistics in this area have been confusing, possibly because reports related the qualifications of the employees, rather than the requirements for the position. To improve comparability in reporting, it is recommended that data be requested in terms of positions rather than of their incumbents. A position can be classified by type with less bias than would prevail if the qualifications and background of the incumbent were considered.

The table calls for the number of vacant positions, in addition to full-time and part-time filled positions, in order to obtain a complete picture of the size of the library operation. It will be noted that figures for the number of building maintenance positions are not requested since they are not considered significant in the evaluation of the library program or in comparing libraries.

Number of Filled and Vacant Positions

	Professional		Nonprofessional (excluding maintenance)
	Librarians	Other	
Full-time positions filled			
Part-time positions filled (in full-time equivalents)			
Vacant positions			

A full-scale manpower study would be required in order to evaluate the quality of staffing in public libraries and to describe the characteristics of library staff members completely. However, it is recommended that the following question be included:

How many library school graduates holding a fifth-year degree in librarianship are on the staff? _____

Salaries of Staff Members. Because library staffs vary so much in size, it is impossible to ask for specific salaries paid. To do so would again raise the problem of the title and definition of the

---

Salaries

of Full-time Professional Staff Members Currently Employed

Instructions: Indicate the number of staff members currently employed in the positions listed according to their present salary brackets. Do not include part-time employees in this table. See glossary for definitions of positions.

	Under $2,000	*$2,000 to $2,999*	*(etc. by $1,000 steps to)*	*$14,000 to $14,999*	*$15,000 and over*
Director (Head Librarian)					
Assistant Director					
Division Head					
Department Head					
Branch Head					
Other supervisory staff					
Nonsupervisory staff					
Library trainee (preprofessional)					

position for which the salary is recorded. Remuneration of librarians, however, is a question which has application beyond just the national issues of manpower and job opportunities. Many libraries use such data when preparing budgets and requesting additional funds. While precise figures may not be obtainable, the salary brackets in the table are detailed enough to be useful for all of these purposes. It should be noted that no distinction is made here between salaries and wages, and that numbers of personnel are meant to represent only full-time staff members. Salaries or wages for part-time staff members would tend to distort interpretation of the table and any derived figures taken from total numbers of staff members and total salaries or wages.

In addition, the following question should be asked:

What is the beginning salary the library offers for
its lowest full-time professional staff position? $_____

System Activities

Statistics are needed which will show the extent and development of interlibrary relationships in activities other than loan of materials, but they are impeded by lack of adequate records and bookkeeping. Questions embodied in the United States Office of Education questionnaire for statistics of public libraries, 1962

Cooperative Activities

Cooperative Services Conducted	Name of Contracting Agencies	Given	Received	Not Applicable
Centralized purchasing				
Centralized cataloging				
Centralized processing				
Revolving book collection				
Shared personnel				
Bookmobile service				
Film circuit				
Reference service				
Bibliographic center service				
Extended borrower's privileges				
Other (specify) _____				

(OE-2001, 8-62), should be continued as a basic approach to this area. Continuing study of emerging system activities should be made with a view toward statistical methods which will reveal trends and evaluate accomplishments. The USOE questions are in the form of a checklist (see preceding table).

In addition, the following checklist should be used to determine presence or absence of other system activities:

1 _____ Audio-visual equipment borrowed
2 _____ Audio-visual equipment lent
3 _____ Book selection service
4 _____ Central storage of little-used materials
5 _____ Consultant service
6 _____ Delivery service
7 _____ In-service training program
8 _____ Poster and display service
9 _____ Public relations and publicity service
10 _____ Return of books to any library in system
11 _____ Uniform borrower's card
12 _____ Union catalog, complete (author, title, subject)
13 _____ Union catalog (adult nonfiction only)
14 _____ Union catalog (adult and juvenile nonfiction)

Income

Statistics relating to public library income are made complex by several factors. First, there is the diversity of sources to which a public library must turn when it is not realistically tax supported. Second, the natural service area may include a combination of separate governmental units which share the cost of public library service. Third, system activities and cooperative practices may involve contracts for specific services rendered. Fourth, as supplemental state grants become more prevalent, more detailed accounting is invariably called for, especially under those state-aid programs which involve matching local funds.

Any questionnaire which covers the more complicated situations will seem overly-detailed to small libraries and to those which derive most funds from a single source. It is better to err on the side of too much detail, however, than too little. Whenever the question does not apply, a notation to this effect can be made.

There is another factor which constantly tends to expand questionnaires. Any set of questions which aims at a grand total must list enough examples to give the librarian the opportunity of entering all pertinent data. Quite often the only way to make a particular question complete is to fragment it into a number of component units which can be summarized into the item sought.

Broad problem areas and trends which are matters of current and national professional concern also influence library questionnaires. Relationships between school districts and public libraries, for example, bear upon the area of student use of public libraries. Data regarding financial assistance from school districts, therefore, should be included. The trend of United Fund organizations to disengage themselves from public-library support presents another example. The questionnaire should provide data which can be used to measure this trend.

The following questions are designed to take these various factors and interests into account. One area, that of income in kind (free rent and utilities, staff members paid by another agency, the value of volunteer-staff time, gift books and subscriptions to periodicals), has not been asked because of the difficulty in determining values and because this area of support does not pass through the library's accounting process.

Income by Source

1 Income from Municipalities[3]
  Direct property or other tax levy
  Appropriation of local tax funds
  Tax funds for contractual services
2 Income from School Districts
  Direct school district tax levy
  Appropriation of school district funds
  School district funds for contractual services
3 Income from Federal and State Grants
  Federal grants
  State grants
  State funds for contractual services
4 Income from Libraries and Other Agencies for Contractual Services
5 Enterprise Income
  Rent of buildings or parts of buildings owned by the library
  Interest or realized gain on investments and endowments
6 Gifts/Donations for Operating Budget
  Community Chest (United Fund)
  Friends of the library

---

[3]Cities, towns, townships, counties, other units of local government.

   Association membership dues
   Individual cash gifts/donations
 7 Petty Cash Income[4]
   Fines, fees,[5] charges for lost books, reserve postals, etc.
   Rental book collection
   Sale of publications
 8 Miscellaneous Income
   Interest on deposits
   Refunds
   Other (specify)

   _____

   _____

 9 *Total Receipts*
10 Unexpended Balance from Previous Year[4]
11 Gifts/Donations for Capital Budget
   Building fund
   Investment/endowment
   Other
12 *Grand Total Receipts*

Expenditures

Statistical reporting of library expenditures must be approached from the standpoint of measuring library programs rather than that of trying to satisfy a certified public accountant. The latter approach is that of an annual report which accounts to the public for the public funds entrusted to the library. Quite often its format will be determined by the particular types and forms of the sources of income, or in the case of "municipal" libraries, by the form in which other municipal expenditures are reported. For statistical purposes, however, expenditures should be reported in such a way as to provide comparison between libraries, and should give data which can be correlated with other statistics. In many instances a particular expenditure, for book stock as an example, when compared with another statistical item, that of number of volumes added, provides added insight into the library's program. Statistics should also provide internal means for double-checking and elucidation. Both of these functions are served by data on expenditures.

In the following table, the arrangement and the individual items are admittedly traditional despite considerable inquiry as

---

[4]Report only if *not* turned into treasury of appropriating unit.
[5]Charges for photocopy service, for example.

to whether this standard approach produces the maximum useful information. Reporting expenditures by program budgeting was considered. Under this method, all costs of a given service (binding, for example) would be grouped together and would show costs of all the staff time, supplies, equipment, and contractual services which are connected with binding. If this were done, the total costs of personnel or library materials would not be available. The reporting librarian would be required to determine how much of a staff member's time is devoted to binding as against other duties. In small or medium-sized libraries such prorating is extremely difficult and frustrating. Program budgeting may be valid and necessary for certain special studies when it can actually be done on a "case study" basis, but it is felt to be impractical and unreasonable on a national, recurring basis. Furthermore, it conflicts with several national standards which cite the proportion of total budget spent for all staff services as against other areas of expenditures.

The number of questions within each broad category of expenditures in the table has been reduced to just those which can reasonably be asked each year without requiring extensive searching of records. The table is intended to serve as a uniform format for all public libraries regardless of size.

An item which does not appear in the table is "Expenditures for Contractual Services." Such an item could be asked as a separate category or could be divided and asked within each broad category of "Personnel," "Library Materials," and "Miscellaneous." While an item for expenditures for contractual services would reveal the extent to which a library depends upon other agencies for certain services, it would not give any new information regarding the essential library program. In some cases, the library's program would even be concealed because the service contracted for would not be identified. This is particularly noticeable if the library contracts for processed books. The item for contractual services would contain (and thus bury) much of the library's book budget. It is recommended, therefore, that contractual services be incorporated within the appropriate accounts. If the contract is for professional staff services, the expenditure would be incorporated within "Library personnel." If it is for already-processed books, the cost of the contracted service will be part of "Book stock."

There are admitted disadvantages to this handling of expenditures for contractual services. It can be argued that the cost of cataloged, classified, and prepared books (complete with catalog cards) is not comparable to the pure cost of books before processing within the library. The one includes personnel, supplies, and overhead costs; the other does not. While this is true, the difficulty of determining the pure book cost of processed books, along with the personnel and other costs involved in the processing, and the assignment of each of these costs to the proper category, is similar to the problems of program budgeting, and has been avoided for the same reasons.

Problems of double-counting of expenditures for contractual services must also be considered. Library "A," for example, will list as an expenditure the funds it has paid to Library "B" for a service rendered. Library "B's" total expenditures will include these same funds as they are expended for staff, supplies, and overhead for the service rendered to Library "A."

This double-counting of funds can be minimized by adjusting total income and expenditure figures of the two libraries. The expenditure should be counted at the library which purchases the service (Library "A")—in other words, where it represents expenditure of local funds. Income from contracts for services should be subtracted from Library "B's" total expenditures in order to compensate. Such adjustments would have to be made at the local or state level, however, because the contracting parties would have to be identified, a process which would be unmanageable on a national scale.

Accurate statistical data on expenditures for contractual services will continue to be unobtainable at the state or national level until some uniform accounting and bookkeeping system is devised and put into practice. It is recommended that a special study aimed at standardization of library bookkeeping and accounting be undertaken at an early date.

Operating Expenditures

1 Expenditures for Personnel
  Library personnel
  Maintenance personnel
  Other personnel costs (e.g., social security, retirement/ pension)
  Total Personnel Costs
2 Expenditures for Library Materials
  Book stock (If *initial* library materials, this fact should be pointed out in a footnote.)

Periodicals collection
Audio-visual materials
Other nonbook materials
Total Library Materials Costs
3 Expenditures for Binding and Rebinding
4 Expenditures for Maintenance of Plant
(to include total for:)

Heat	Operation and maintenance of vehicles
Light	Equipment repairs and replacement
Power	Furnishings repairs and replacement
Water	Building repairs and redecoration
Telephone	Maintenance of grounds

5 Fixed Charges and Debt Service (to include total for:)
Rent
Amortization of long-term debts
Interest on all loans, long and short term
Insurance (all except F.I.C.A.)
6 Expenditures for Supplies and Miscellaneous
(to include total for:)
Stationery and supplies

Printing and advertising	Travel
Photocopying costs	Memberships
Repairing and mending	Other

Postage, freight, express
7 Total Operating Expenditures
8 Adjustment (Subtract income from libraries for contractual services listed in item 4 of *Income by Source*)
9 Total Operating Expenditures—Adjusted

Capital Expenditures

10 Capital Expenditures (excluding additions to endowment funds and other investments for capital gain) to include total for:
Building sites
New buildings and additions to existing buildings: major structural changes, with architect's fees, permits, etc.
Furnishings and equipment for new or expanded quarters
Additional furnishings and equipment for existing buildings
11 Total Expenditures, Operating and Capital

Expenditures for Personnel. All costs of staff services appear as a unified category which includes an item for social security and pension/retirement payments. In many cases a breakdown of expenditures for library personnel into "professional personnel" and "nonprofessional personnel" would be useful. Because this questionnaire would go to "one-man libraries" as well as to those with sizeable staffs, this amount of detail is not recommended. To do so would require the librarian in the small agency to pro-rate his time between professional and clerical duties. Review of tables concerned with numbers of staff (see "Personnel," p.48), and salary brackets by category of staff member, will give some measure as to proportion of expenditures for *professional vs. nonprofessional* library personnel.

Expenditures for Library Materials. Categories here conform to the broad categories of library holdings (i.e., book stock, periodicals collection, nonbook materials) for correlation with those statistics. The definitions of these categories will be essential to correct reporting, and the glossary should be consulted. Cost of audio-visual materials, although a point of detail within nonbook materials, is included as a separate account because of widespread interest in this field. In accordance with counting procedures already discussed, expenditures for book stock in microform would be included here.

Expenditures for Binding and Rebinding. Because of factors mentioned before, almost the entire expenditure reported in this category will generally represent payments to a commercial binder, and will not include the staff and materials costs of work done at the library. If the library operates its own bindery (as is the case with some very large libraries) this fact will be brought out in the question under "Technical Services," p.48. It is possible in these cases that the expenditure would include personnel and supplies costs, but this should not impede comparison with binding expenditures of other libraries, provided those costs are not counted again under "Personnel" and "Supplies."

If the pattern of expenditures for "staff," "library materials," and "other" is preferred, expenditures for binding would be added with that of library materials.

Other Operating Expenditures. It is recommended that the usual category of "other operating expenditures" be subdivided into three parts which appear in the table as:

4 Expenditures for Maintenance of Plant
5 Fixed Charges and Debt Service
6 Expenditures for Supplies and Miscellaneous

There are several reasons for subdividing the catch-all category of "other operating expenditures." First, the three subdivisions with their explanatory notes assure the inclusion of the item desired and the exclusion of those not desired. Second, they provide grouping of items within meaningful categories and facilitate the comparison of library operations and programs. Third, they clarify the difference between operating and capital expenditures.

In this last regard, it will be noted that costs of repairing and replacing already-existing furnishings and equipment are considered "operating," and that costs of additional furnishings and equipment not already owned by the library are considered "capital." "Maintenance of Plant" is taken to include all those costs necessary to keeping the building fully operative and in good condition. Detail as to individual items in this category is not necessary—one total figure will suffice. Replacement of items by means of a depreciation allowance, however, will be counted under "Capital Expenditures" when the funds are actually expended.

Within the item for "Fixed Charges and Debt Service" a library would report the costs of rent if it does not own the building(s), or the cost of an amortized mortgage if it is purchasing the building over a period of time. In the one case, the expenditure will result in increased assets; in the other, it will not. The purpose of these library statistics, however, is to illustrate the library's program, not to record assets and liabilities. The expenditures are comparable since their purpose is the same, namely, to pay for use of the facilities.

One point regarding payments of loans should be clarified. A short-term loan, borrowed and paid back within the same fiscal period, should not be reflected in financial statistics, either as income when borrowed or expenditure when repaid. Reporting such transactions inflates and distorts a library's financial data. Interest on such loans, however, should be reported as an operating expenditure. If the library is operating "in the red," a comparison of total income with total expenditures will reveal this fact. However, these totals need not be exactly balanced as in a treasurer's or accountant's report.

"Expenditures for Supplies and Miscellaneous" are self-explanatory and need not be reported individually. If special study is needed on a particular detail within this category, a special questionnaire could be designed.

Capital Expenditures. Only those expenditures which increase the library's service or capacity to serve should be included in the total figure called for under "Capital Expenditures." Additions made to the endowment fund, the building fund, the savings fund, the sinking fund, and depreciation allowances should be excluded from this item, as should investments made in securities or real estate which are intended to increase the library's income. Statistics on library expenditures should show how much is being spent on library *service* rather than how much is being spent on library *security*. When, for example, the money which has been set aside in a depreciation allowance is *actually* expended, it would be counted as a capital expenditure.

The subject of library endowments and investments should be treated as a special study, with questions designed specifically for the purposes of such a study. If it is believed that reporting libraries would confuse expenditures for library service (both operating and capital) with those for future service (i.e., investments for more income or savings toward a new building or particular project), a table could be added.

Statistics of

State Library Agencies

Types of Library Services

Comparative statistics of library functions at the state level have been all but nonexistent in the past, and thus current practice cannot be delineated and coordinated with other library statistics. The opportunity for a fresh approach to the problem has many advantages. The recent publication of *Standards for Library Functions at the State Level* (American Library Association, 1963) represents a milestone in clarifying those library functions which are thought to be essential for any state. To determine how far each state is from the desired level represented in the *Standards* would be one of the objectives of the stabilization of future state library statistics.

A state library may be defined as a library maintained by state funds for the use of state government, libraries throughout the state, and usually for all citizens, either directly or through their local libraries. However, this definition, adapted from the *A.L.A. Glossary of Library Terms,* does little to separate "state library agencies" from the multitude of special libraries serving state government. Nor would one suspect the great variation which exists among state library agencies in the United States. One state may have all main state-library functions under a single administrative unit; another may have extension functions placed within its education department, a separate law library, a legislative reference service attached to the legislature, and so on. In Maryland the state library's general collections exist by virtue of a contract with the Enoch Pratt Free Library of Baltimore.

Because the various state library services are seldom administered by one central agency, the phrase "library functions at the state level" is increasingly in use. The approach taken in the *Standards* is that of identifying the various services which should exist within a state and for which the state should take some responsibility. This responsibility may be exercised by providing library service directly, promoting service through other agencies, and coordinating the various library resources, with state financial aid and regulatory requirements serving as levers for library development. Central administration of the services, however, is not a requisite.

It is necessary first to identify the principal functions of state library service, then to determine whether a state provides all or part of them and through what administrative framework. Taken in the aggregate, these functions form the state library service, regardless of whether they are performed by one distinct unit, are attached to several state agencies, or are contracted for by the state.

State library services may be thought of in a number of broad categories: general library services, historical library services, documents depository services, law library services, legislative reference services, extension (library development) services, and others (such as services to the visually handicapped, medical library services, etc.). Excluded from present consideration are archival services, which, although covered in the *Standards,* do not lend themselves to comparative statistical measurement. It is felt that state archives collections and services should be subjects of special study.

General Library Services. Most states maintain for the use of state government and the public at large a collection of library materials spanning the broad areas of knowledge. The *Standards* indicate that such a collection "should include not only books, but research and information reports; journals of trade, industrial and professional groups; files of state and major national newspapers; maps and similar materials." Included within the subject resources of this general collection should be "a comprehensive collection on present and potential state policies and state responsibilities."

The general collection of state library agencies forms part of, and reinforces, the total library resources of the state. On the one hand, it is designed to support general library needs of all residents of the state and should be included in any measurement of total public library resources. On the other hand, it is designed to support special library service to particular clienteles, especially the various branches of state government.

This dual public/special role presents problems to the statistician seeking to report the total activity of a state or of the nation by type of library. It is recommended that the total library resources of the agencies making up the state library, and the total cost and use of them, be reported as part of the total public library service of the state and nation, since the public has either direct access to the collections or indirect access through local libraries.

Taken in the broadest sense, the general library collection is the composite of holdings of all the several agencies carrying out the library functions at the state level. Thus, state law libraries, documents depositories, state history collections, etc., which are designed for the general public as well as state office service, can be thought of as subject departments of the general library collection. Statistics for these collections should be grouped together whether or not they are administratively tied together, and should be reflected in totals for the state library agencies' resources, staff, and services. Also to be included are any auxiliary agencies (permanent branches and other services outlets of the state library agency) and any collections maintained by the state through contract with nonstate governmental libraries (such as materials for the visually handicapped).

Excluded from the totals for state library agencies would be those resources and services of state departments and agencies for which the state library has no responsibility, those not designed for general public use, and those not represented in a catalog to which the general public has access. Among such collections one might find, for example, the working collection of legal materials in the Justice Department (as distinguished from the law library); libraries in state correctional institutions and state institutions of higher education; special scientific and technological collections within such agencies as the State Geological Survey, Department of Health, etc. If, however, any of these collections were administered by that agency which is identified as the State Library, or open for general public use, statistics for them should be included.

Within the total subject holdings which form the library functions at the state level are certain resources which are singled out in the *Standards* and often exist as distinct "libraries" in the state library complex. If one of the purposes of statistics is to reflect the extent to which the state agencies approach the standards, these areas will have to be identified statistically, even though grouped with the general collection and totaled together. Separate records are usually maintained; if not, the total would have to suffice.

Historical Library Services. The *Standards* point out that "a strong collection of history related to the state—regional, state and local" should be maintained. In some states such a history collection may be maintained by the state but might not be administered as part of the state library's general library collection. Figures should be gathered which will reveal such collections and services. They should be included in state library totals— but only as long as the service is primarily supported by the state. Library collections and services of state historical societies (i.e., agencies not administered by state government) of course are not to be counted as part of state library collections.

Law Library Services. The holdings of primary and secondary legal materials of the state (maintained for the judicial, legislative, and executive branches of state government and for the lower courts, attorneys, and law students) constitute a special library resource and service within the state library framework. As state supported services, they may also be made available to interested citizens, and in some cases may actually constitute a subject department within the general library services. Statistics for law library services should be identified and included with totals for state library agencies. While the size, cost, and use of the law collection will thus be counted in total public library statistics of the state, the collection should also be identified in directories and indexes of special libraries, and in statistics incorporated in any state or national summary of special law library services.

Documents Depository Services. The systematic collection and servicing of a state's documents (and those of other states, the federal government, and foreign governments) is a state library function. Statistics of such a collection, wherever it falls within the state governmental structure, should be identified and included with those of other state library functions, and thus with the total public library resources and services of the states. If regional, state-documents depositories are maintained by the state, this fact should be brought out under "other agencies of service, branches, etc." If holdings of regional depositories are included with central-collection statistics, a footnote should point this out. Nonstate governmental libraries which are designated as regional documents depositories should not be counted here.

Other Services. This category is needed to cover library services to the blind and services such as the medical library administered by the New York State Library. The same principles mentioned before as to whether the service comes within the general framework of the state library agency should be applied.

Legislative Reference Services. Although the acquisition of materials and staff to provide research and special information services for the state legislature is a natural function of the general library services of a state library, this activity is often assigned to a separate agency and coupled with nonlibrary services. Sometimes the agency provides bill drafting and indexing, and considers itself apart from the state library agency. If this is the case and the collection of library materials held by the legislative reference agency is primarily a working collection, such an agency would be thought of as one of the many special libraries serving state governments. Statistics would not be included in state library totals.

Extension Services (Library Development Services). Extension service, within the broadest library context, generally entails the supplying of books and library services to individuals or organizations outside a library's regular service area. Within this concept (adapted from the definition in the *A.L.A. Glossary of Library Terms*) would come interlibrary loan and reference services, off-campus services of college and university libraries, and deposit collections of public libraries within schools and institutions.

When speaking of state library functions, however, the word *extension* takes on a certain characteristic meaning. The service would include advisory services, promotion of library service, supervision of projects supported with state or federal funds, and statistical and other research activities which will reveal the level of library services available and needed within the state. The term "library development" is increasingly used to cover these activities. In many instances the extension or library development agency maintains a book collection which is placed on deposit with county, public school, and institutional libraries and circulated through state-owned bookmobiles. When it is maintained as a central collection, it may form the resource for extension reference services and interlibrary loans. These resources and services should be identified and included in total statistics of the state library and of public library activity in the state.

Overlapping with Other Types of Libraries

Although the foregoing paragraphs place state library functions as part of the total *public* library service of a state, some of the library activities at the state level should be included in summaries of special library service and school library service.

Special Libraries. It has been mentioned that the law library service at the state level should be reflected in directories of special libraries in general and in statistics of law libraries in particular. Other special collections and services of state libraries should be listed in special directories (e.g., archives, state history, genealogy). But whenever the collection and the service is open to the public, the resources and services of the collection should be counted with total public library statistics. Specialized working collections in divisions and agencies of state government probably will continue to be thought of as special libraries even though they may be developed under the administration of, or in close coordination with, the central state library agency.

School Libraries. "The function of advising and supervising school libraries should normally be placed in the agency concerned directly with elementary and secondary schools in the Department of Education" (*Standards,* #38). Despite this clear statement, or perhaps more properly as a causative for it, some state libraries or state library extension agencies have legal responsibilities for school libraries. In such cases, statistics relating to resources and services maintained for school library development should be included in the state summary of school library services rather than in any state summary of public library services.

State Library Statistics by Category

The following questions and tables are an attempt to identify specific statistical data regarding state library activities and resources which are significant on a national level. Details regarding most items have already been presented in the preceding section on public library statistics and are not repeated here.

The present attempt to devise a state library questionnaire was felt to be necessary for the purposes and aims of this Project, even though it tends to duplicate or anticipate the efforts of several other groups.[1] Since it is one of the first attempts in this area and has not been tested, the questions and the arrangement of the tables should be considered only a point of departure for future study.

Collections. Quantities of some library materials are difficult to determine, and detailed reporting of all the major service-points carrying out library functions at the state level would be cumbersome. Quantitative measures have therefore been restricted. The number of volumes lost or withdrawn is not asked because this level of detail is not needed annually. The research nature of state library collections will tend to minimize active weeding programs.

Income. The question of state library income has for many years been academic; but since the Library Services Act, considerable sums of federal money have gone into operating and strengthening state library agencies. The following questions attempt to identify state and federal funds and any other sources of income which are used for operating the various services of the state library agency.

---

[1](a) U. S. Office of Education, Library Services Division, *Survey of Special Libraries Serving State Governments* (in progress).

(b) Statistics Committee for State Libraries (American Library Association, Library Organization and Management Section).

(c) Phillip Monypenny and others, *Survey of Library Functions of the States* (A.L.A., unpublished study).

Agencies of Service

Identification, Organization

1 Official name of state library agency
2 Address
3 Name and title of person in charge
4 Name of department, board, commission, or agency in which administratively placed
5 Title of person or name of board to whom person in charge reports
6 Is there a library advisory committee or board that has been constituted for the purpose of guiding or advising the state library agency?
7 If so, name of such committee or board

8 *State Library Function*	*Check if administered by state library agency*	*If not administered by state library agency, give name and address of agency responsible for the function*
General Library collection	_____	_____
Historical Library services	_____	_____
Documents Depository (state, local, federal, U.N., etc.)	_____	_____
Law Library	_____	_____
Other (Medical Library, Services for the blind, etc. Specify:)	_____	_____
	_____	_____
Legislative Reference service	_____	_____
Library Development (Extension) services	_____	_____

9 Number of branches maintained throughout the state
10 Number of deposit stations maintained throughout the state
11 Number of bookmobiles operated from the state agency

Collections

Basic Collections

	Gen-eral	His-tory	Docu-ments	Law Lib.	Other‡	Legis-lative Ref.	Exten-sion Svc.	Total
1 Book Stock:								
Total volumes*		†	†					
No. added this year								
2 Periodicals Collection:								
No. periodicals titles currently received								
No. newspapers titles currently received								
No. periodicals held (biblio-graphic vols.)								
No. newspapers held (biblio-graphic vols.)								
3 Audio-Visual Materials:								
No. films								
No. recordings								

*Documents (in the fourth column) would be counted by item rather than volume and should exclude material which is to be superseded by permanent cumulative editions.

†Enter separate figures here (1) if these collections are administered by the state library agency, and (2) if they are not included within figures for the General Library Collection.

‡Separate collections administered by the state library agency such as medical library, library service to the blind, etc., should be identified in the table on page 68 and here as well. Additional columns might be necessary.

Circulation

Basic Collections

	Gen-eral	His-tory	Docu-ments	Law Lib.	Other	Legis-lative Ref.	Exten-sion Svc.	Total
1 Circulation (total no. of items)								
2 Interlibrary Loans: Total items lent								
Total items borrowed								
3 Photocopy Service (total no. supplied in lieu of circulation)								
4 Reference Service (no. of transactions)								

Personnel

Basic Collections

	General	History	Documents	Law Lib.	Other	Legislative Ref.	Extension Svc.	Total
1 No. of filled positions (full-time equiv.):								
Librarians								
Other Professionals								
Nonprofessionals								
Total Filled Positions								
2 No. of budgeted positions vacant (full-time equiv.):								
Librarians								
Other Professionals								
Nonprofessionals								
3 Total Staff Complement (filled and vacant positions, full-time equiv.)								

Salaries/Wages

Salaries/Wages of Full-time Professional Staff Members Currently Employed
(exclusive of building maintenance staff)

Instructions: Indicate the number of professional staff members currently
employed in the positions listed, according to the salary/wages bracket into
which their present salaries/wages fall. Do not include part-time employees.

	Under $5,000	*$5,000-$5,999*	*$6,000-$6,999*	*(etc. in thousands up to)*	*$14,000-$14,999*	*$15,000 & over*
1 Administration:						
Director of State Library						
Assistant Director						
Head, General Library						
Head, History						
Head, Documents						
Head, Law Library						
Head, Legislative Ref.						
Head, Extension Services						
2 Other Supervisory Staff:						
Field Consultants						
Other (specify)						
_____						
_____						
3 Nonsupervisory Professional Personnel						
4 Library Trainees (preprofessional)						

In addition, the following question should be asked:

What is the salary the state library agency offers its beginning
(lowest) professional staff member?

Income

	State Funds*	Federal Funds†	Other‡	Total
General Library Services				
Historical Library Services				
Documents Depository Services				
Law Library Services				
Other (specify)				
Legislative Reference				
Extension Services				
Totals				

*State appropriations for operating expenditures. Exclude funds appropriated for grants-in-aid.

†Include only federal funds used for operating and strengthening the state library agency. Do not include demonstration grants made to other libraries or funds expended for contractual services.

‡The sources of these funds should be cited through footnoting.

Expenditures

	Gen-eral	His-tory	Docu-ments	Law Lib.	Other	Legis-lative Ref.	Exten-sion Svc.	Total

Operating Expenditures
1 Staff Costs:

Library personnel
Maintenance personnel*
Other personnel costs*
(FICA, retirement, etc.)
Total

2 Library Materials:

Book Stock
Periodicals Collection
Audio-Visual Materials
Other library materials
Total

3 Other Operating Expenditures†

4 Contractual Services‡

5 Total Operating Expenditures

Capital Expenditures§

6 Additional Equipment

7 Bookmobiles, Other Vehicles

8 Other (specify)

9 Total Capital Expenditures

Total Operating and Capital Expenditures

*Include only if funds are expended from the state library agency's operating budget.
†This item would normally cover supplies, replacement or repair of equipment, etc., and is not intended to cover expenditures for maintenance of plant which may not be charged to the state library agency's operating budget.
‡Do not include here any expenditures for staff, library materials, or others which are included above.
§Expenditures for land, new buildings, and major additions to buildings are usually financed through a "general state authority," and are therefore not included.

Summary

Total Expenditures Administered by State Library Agency

1 Total operating and capital expenditures for state
library agency (carried forward from
preceding table) $_____
2 State grants administered by state library agency for:
Public libraries $_____
School libraries $_____
Libraries for the visually handicapped $_____
Other libraries (specify) $_____
Scholarships for library trainees $_____
Contracts for research in librarianship $_____
Other grants (specify) $_____
3 Federal grants administered by state library agency
(not included with state funds above) $_____
4 Total expenditures administered by
state library agency $_____

Other State Library Activities

There are a number of activities of state library agencies which will bear occasional but detailed study. In many instances not enough is known of them to ask pertinent quantitative questions, and until more data can be obtained, it is recommended that only presence or absence of the following activities be determined.

Does the state library agency administer:

1 Certification of public librarians
2 In-service training institutes or workshops for:
   Personnel in professional library positions
   Personnel in nonprofessional library positions
   Library trustees
   Other (specify: e.g., school administrators, etc.)
3 Scholarships/stipends for attendance at:
   Workshops/institutes
   Library schools for degree programs
   Library courses for credit or certification but not for a degree
4 Centralized technical services for public libraries:
   Centralized purchasing
   Centralized cataloging
   Centralized physical preparation of books for the shelf
5 Union catalog
6 Revolving book collections
7 Deposit collections in public libraries
8 Bookmobile service
9 Film circuits
10 Central storage for little-used materials
11 Poster and display service
12 Public relations and publicity services for public libraries
13 Placement service for public library staff members

V

Statistics of
School Libraries

Part One
SCHOOLS

The need for school library statistics is generated at five separate levels and for many different, though related, uses. The most basic statistical records are maintained and used in individual schools and in school systems to measure growth and progress in school library programs, and to justify requests for appropriations for materials, personnel, quarters and equipment, and supplies. State departments of education collect school library statistics often as a part of general school or school system reports both for publication in education department reports and for use in accreditation or approval programs. The State Department of Education, if it collects school library statistics, usually gathers them from all public schools or school systems in the state. Regional accreditation associations, on the other hand, collect information only from individual schools. These associations evaluate the reports submitted for accreditation purposes, but usually do not publish the data. The fifth level, the U.S. Office of Education, collects school library statistics on a national basis.

Units of Enumeration for School Library Statistics

There are two possible basic units for the enumeration of school library statistics, the school and the school system. Local school systems are concerned with measuring the growth and progress of individual school-library programs within their systems by comparing them with similar schools in the local system, the state, and the nation.

The school system, a single taxing authority and a unified administrative organization, appears to provide a logical unit of enumeration for public-school libraries. The system sets common policies for all schools within a system and budgets for them on the basis of common educational goals and programs. School libraries, developed to help achieve these goals, are increasingly supported and staffed on the basis of system-wide policies. Together, they form a system of libraries supporting the common curriculum of a system of schools.

However, most types of school library data are more meaningful if collected on an individual school basis rather than for a system. The number of periodical titles currently received, for example, has little meaning if reported for a school system, but has great value for analyzing the resources of an individual school library. The seating capacity of a library is less meaningful when reported for a school system, since it must be interpreted in terms of the membership of the individual school served by that library. The collection of school library statistics from individual schools will also make it possible to collect library data for nonpublic schools which are not organized into school systems.

It is recommended, therefore, that school library statistics be collected from individual public and nonpublic schools for presentation at both state and national levels.

Type of School Library Service to Be Reported

A school library is a library administered as a unit, usually in one place in the school. Since it makes books and other library materials available to all teachers and pupils in the school, other methods of providing books to students should not be counted as school library service. Detailed information concerning permanent classroom collections of materials, even though such collections are a substitute for school library service, should not be collected as school library statistics. School-system central office libraries, by the same token, may send collections of materials to schools for use by teachers and pupils in classrooms. However, they should not be included with school libraries, since they do not fit the basic school library definition. Their resources and services should be reported separately (see "Part Two").

Similarly, the various types of service to schools provided by public libraries—bookmobile service, classroom loan collections, or a combination of them—should be excluded from school library services. These services, though they make a contribution to the school program, lack essential characteristics of school library service. If reported, they should be used merely to show their existence as a substitute for school libraries.

Libraries located in school buildings, but administered by public libraries, present a special problem. Whether they are public libraries located physically in schools, or school libraries, is a legitimate question, but one that can be answered pragmatically. When a library located in a school, even though administered by a public library, exists primarily to serve the pupils and teachers of the school, it should be counted as a school library. If, however, such a library is intended to serve the general public, and in an incidental way serves the teachers and pupils of the school, it is still essentially a public library and should be counted as one. To be counted as a school library for statistical purposes, a library located in a school but administered by a public library should meet *all* of the following criteria:

1 The librarian must be a certified school librarian under State Department of Education certification regulations.
2 The library must be available for pupil and teacher use throughout the school day.
3 The library collection must be selected to support the school curriculum.

School-housed branch public libraries should be included in public library statistics. On the other hand, a library which gives only incidental service to the general public and is administered by a board of education should be counted as a school library.

Reporting Period

The reporting period for school library statistics is basically the school year. However, since the school year ends on different days in different school systems, the last day of June provides a convenient date for the reporting of data which must be based on a common date for comparability. Information which is cumulative over a period of time can be reported from the preceding July 1 to June 30. This practice has the additional advantage that the reporting period coincides with the fiscal year of most school systems.

Grade Level of Schools Served

Information on school libraries is desirable for schools of all grade levels—elementary schools, junior high schools, high schools or senior high schools, junior-senior high schools, and combined elementary and secondary school plants. The definitions for each level of school have been provided in the glossary. These definitions, adapted from the *Common Core of State Educational Information,* should be used in reporting school library statistics. Statistics for junior college libraries operated by public school systems should be reported with statistics of colleges and universities. In individual school reports, the grade span of the school should be indicated.

Clientele

The clientele of a school library is made up of the pupils, teachers, and other professional staff members of the school, such as principals, consultants or supervisors of instruction, guidance personnel, psychological personnel, and librarians. The number of teachers and of other professional staff members should be reported in terms of full-time equivalents. To provide a complete picture of clientele magnitude and make available more valid derived data (such as per capita costs or volumes per capita), it is recommended that the number of pupils, teachers, and other professional staff members be reported.

Three ways of counting pupils could be used—enrollment, average daily attendance, or average daily membership. Enrollment is least desirable because it changes throughout the school year. Dropouts have not been eliminated, but new enrollees have been added. Both "average daily attendance" and "average daily membership" are more indicative of the number of pupils who must be provided with school library service. Average daily membership is more nearly exact, since it takes into account excused absentees for whom library service would have to be provided if they were present. Although many state departments of education require local school systems to report average daily attendance for state accounting purposes, average daily membership is now quite generally available. For national purposes, it is recommended that average daily membership be reported.

Hours of Service

The hours of service of school libraries provides a measure of the availability of materials to pupils and teachers. The school day, including a half-hour before the beginning of classes and a half-hour after the end of classes, is the traditional period of service of the school library. However, if a school librarian is not present to provide professional services, the question must be asked whether the library is actually available for use in the sense that a full range of services is available. In the case of school libraries, the best answer would seem to be in the affirmative. The presence of a teacher with the pupils assures a measure of advice and guidance so that the library and its collections can be used. Using this interpretation it would be necessary only to report that the library is open for use during the school day, since it could be used by teachers and pupils even though a school librarian was not present. However, do not count those hours during which the library is locked because of the absence of the school librarian.

The use of school libraries during the evening, on Saturdays, and during vacation periods should be reported, since this extended service is an emerging trend of significance in relation to changes in instruction and in the use of materials.

It is recommended that both regular hours of service and extended hours be reported for individual school libraries.

Physical Facilities

Standards for school library facilities usually recommend from 25 to 30 or 35 square feet per reader in school libraries, with sufficient seating capacity to accommodate a specified number of readers or percentage of the school's enrollment. It is recommended that seating capacity be reported.

Two other items of general information are desirable and should also be reported:

The total area of the library in square feet
The volume capacity of the library

Since school libraries include auxiliary rooms or areas planned to provide for specialized functions or services, their availability is significant in measuring the library services provided. Information on the availability of special areas in school libraries should be collected so that the data gathered can be interpreted in conjunction with the seating capacity of the library, the size of the school, etc. It is recommended that the availability of the following areas or rooms be reported:

Reading rooms
Conference areas
Work room or area

Library classroom
Audio-visual rooms or areas
Area for teacher-preparation of materials
Area for professional library
Exhibit and demonstration areas
Department libraries
Carrels

Library Collection

Information concerning school library collections is of paramount importance as an indication of the ability of the library to meet instructional needs. Collection of statistics for each major type of material in the library's collection is desirable, and certainly for those on which school libraries maintain an inventory or similar record.

Four items of information are useful relative to school library collections:

The number of items on the first day of the reporting period
The number of items added during the reporting period
The number of items withdrawn during the reporting period
The number of items on the last day of the reporting period

These questions can be applied to each of the chief categories of school-library materials, except periodicals.

Book Stock. The current practice in regard to reporting the book collection varies, some jurisdictions asking for the number of titles, others asking the number of volumes, and a few asking both. Reporting the number of volumes is recommended, since it gives a fuller picture of the quantity of material available for the instructional program. The number of duplicates, i.e., the difference between counting titles and volumes, depends on the enrollment of each school, the nature of the curriculum, and the ways in which materials are used; therefore, the need for duplicates is not constant from school to school. The number of titles might be the more useful figure for small schools where achieving an adequate range of material is more crucial and more difficult. In practice, duplication of titles decreases almost to the vanishing point in very small schools, so that volumes and titles are almost synonomous.

Some state and regional accrediting associations collect information concerning the percentage of the collection in each broad category of the Dewey Decimal Classification and set standards accordingly. This practice, useful for evaluating the library of an individual school, is not recommended for state and national statistics programs.

Separate reporting of fiction and nonfiction cannot be considered useful, since in school libraries both are acquired for curricular and educational purposes.

Periodicals and Newspapers. The number of periodical and newspaper subscriptions currently received, excluding duplicates, should be reported separately for individual school libraries. Some states collect lists of titles received, but it is difficult to see a practical use for such detailed information, since it can be evaluated only in terms of a careful analysis of the school's curriculum. Identification of duplicates would add little to the knowledge of library holdings.

Information concerning holdings of back volumes of periodicals, bound and unbound, should be reported by bibliographic volumes as indicated by the publisher. Though school library practice has not encouraged building long runs of back volumes in the past, changes in school library use resulting from recent curriculum advances will probably lead school libraries to maintain larger periodicals collections in the future. Reporting these collections will provide information needed for evaluating the school library's ability to meet the needs of students. Back volumes should be reported under three categories:

Number of bound volumes
Number of unbound volumes
Number of volumes on microfilm

Nonbook Materials. Collections of films, filmstrips, tape recordings, disc recordings, slides, transparencies, and other audiovisual materials are extensive enough in school libraries to warrant reporting. These materials should be reported by physical item—reel, disc, or frame. The number at the beginning of the reporting period, number added and number withdrawn during the reporting period, and the number at the end of the reporting period should be indicated for each type of material.

Pictures and other vertical-file materials, while important in school library collections, are not usually inventoried or cataloged individually. Other than indicating the availability of such collections, no counting is recommended for school reports.

Microform. Since microform materials are being used increasingly, especially in high-school libraries, it is desirable that these materials be reported by physical item, using the four categories used for book stock and for nonbook materials. Periodicals on microfilm will be reported twice, but will not be totaled.

Library Use

Circulation and Reference Service. Reporting of circulation and reference service of the library presents special problems. Circulation practices differ widely from school to school in such aspects as length of loans and renewal policy. As a result, figures for one school are often not comparable with others. For this reason, it is recommended that circulation figures not be reported.

Similar factors lead to the same recommendation for reference service of the school library. It is frequently difficult to differentiate between reference assistance and reader guidance, for example. A new teacher planning a unit may seek assistance his first year, but when teaching the same unit in subsequent years, is able to find the same material for himself. He may be making reference use of material in both cases, but only the first is reported. Reporting only questions asked of the librarian is, at best, only a partial record of reference use of the library. In the school library, class instruction in the use of materials may remove the need for numerous reference questions. Reporting questions asked will not demonstrate the magnitude of reference service.

Other Services. Other services of the school library, such as lessons in library use, book talks, storytelling, and so forth, represent qualitative aspects of school library programs. Important as they are in effective school library service, they do not lend themselves to statistical treatment. They should be the subject of special studies rather than of regular school-library statistics surveys.

Personnel

Number of Library Staff Positions. Both professional and nonprofessional school library personnel should be reported. Since volunteer student assistants do not, individually, contribute large amounts of time to school library service, there is serious doubt that regular reporting of student assistants adds to information concerning personnel serving school libraries. As the use of paid student assistants grows, there may be value in reporting the number of hours they work.

Statistics for school librarians should include:

The number of school librarians

The number of credits in library education of school librarians

The salaries of school librarians

The number of school librarians with fifth-year degrees in library science

Defining a school librarian is most controversial. While the school library profession, in general, recommends a relatively high number of semester hours of library education as the basic minimum qualification for school librarians, certification requirements are markedly different from state to state, ranging from as few as 6 semester hours to as many as 36. For statistical purposes, state practice would seem to have precedence over professional opinion. Adopting a higher figure for the library-education requirements of school librarians is a matter for state action rather than for definition in a statistical handbook. Collecting information which shows how many school librarians have a given amount of library education will reveal the current situation and provide data needed for state action. It is recommended that school librarians be reported by number of semester hours in library education, excluding from reporting as librarians any with fewer hours than any state recognizes. This would exclude teachers with fewer than six semester hours of library education who have been assigned to library service, but should not be interpreted as defining the amount of library education desirable.

Teachers with fewer than six semester hours of library education who have been assigned to school libraries should be reported separately in order to provide a complete record of personnel engaged in school library service. Other professional personnel, such as audio-visual specialists and subject specialists assigned to school library service, should also be reported by number and type of positions.

Because many school librarians serve less than full time, a problem exists in reporting numbers of school librarians. It is recommended that part-time school librarians be reported in full-time equivalents. This method of reporting would provide a more nearly accurate basis for such derived statistics as librarian-pupil ratio. Itinerant librarians who serve more than one school should be reported as part-time employees in individual school reports.

Nonprofessional personnel should be reported in the same

manner, converting part-time employees into full-time equivalents. This would provide an accurate reporting of the amount of clerical and other nonprofessional personnel serving school libraries.

It is recommended that volunteer adult workers in school libraries not be reported in recurring statistical surveys. Usually a large number of such workers contribute a very small amount of time each. If numbers of people are reported, the totals are unduly inflated in terms of the quality of service provided.

Salaries of Full-time Professional Staff Members. School-library staff salaries should be reported by steps of $1,000 within the range from $3,000 to $9,999 (e.g., $3,000–3,999, $4,000–4,999, etc.), indicating the number of full-time professional staff members whose salaries fall in each bracket. The following position breakdown is recommended:

> Head librarian
> Assistant librarians
> Other professional personnel

For comparability purposes, salaries of school librarians and other professional personnel should be reported separately for 10-, 11-, and 12-month employment periods. Contributed services, the monetary value of work performed by members of religious orders, should be equated with salaries paid to lay staff and reported separately.

Expenditures

Information concerning total costs of school library service is not currently available on a national basis, but would have value in planning school library programs. It is recommended that data concerning school library expenditures be collected in school library statistics surveys.

Operating Expenditures. Operating expenditures for school libraries fall into clear-cut categories and are relatively easily reported. The reporting of income, however, is not too significant for these reasons:

> Total expenditures would provide a reasonable approximation of total income since appropriated funds are usually not carried over from one fiscal period to another.
> The great bulk of school library funds of any given school originate at a single source.

However, if funds have been received as gifts, for example, from parent-teacher organizations or from other sources, they should also be reported as part of the money expended.

Expenditures should be reported for each of the following items:

Salaries of library staff
  Salaries of professional personnel
  Salaries of nonprofessional personnel
Expenditures for books
Expenditures for periodicals and newspapers
Expenditures for audio-visual materials
Expenditures for binding and rebinding
Other expenditures, such as maintenance of equipment, supplies, etc.

In reporting salaries of personnel who work less than full time, only that portion of the total salary which represents the fraction of the individual's work load devoted to library service should be reported.

Some states require separate reporting of expenditures for encyclopedias. Since encyclopedias are part of the book collection, it is recommended that they be included with book expenditures.

Problems arise in comparability with respect to expenditures for supplies in school systems which provide centralized processing—services representing a large portion of the supplies budget. The expenditures for these supplies should be reported as part of the school-system central office budget (see "Part Two").

It is recommended that each of the above expenditures be reported for individual school libraries.

Capital Expenditures.[1] Three types of expenditures should be reported separately as capital expenditures for school libraries:

Expenditures for audio-visual equipment
Expenditures for library furniture and equipment
Expenditures for the initial purchase of books for a new school library, or large accessions involving an expansion of the library

Separate reporting of these capital items will help provide a

---

[1]Capital expenditures categories used in this section are based on *Financial Accounting for Local and State School Systems,* State Educational Records and Reports Series: Handbook II, Bulletin 1957, No. 4 (Washington: U.S. Department of Health, Education, and Welfare, Office of Education, 1957).

clearer picture of the costs of school library services. Building costs, which are a part of the cost of the entire school, should not be reported.

Part Two
SCHOOL-SYSTEM CENTRAL OFFICES

To present a more nearly complete picture of library services, school library statistical programs should include recurring studies of library services provided by school-system central offices. The services reported should include the following:

School system materials centers which lend materials and/or equipment to schools, including professional libraries for teachers, and curriculum materials laboratories
School library supervision
School-system central processing centers

Information concerning these central office services could not be collected on the same forms as school library data, but would require separate questionnaires to be completed at the school system level, rather than by individual schools.

School-System Materials Centers

School-system materials centers, professional libraries, and curriculum materials laboratories should be reported together, whether they are administratively unified or not, since much of the general information relating to them is the same.

Clientele. The clientele of school-system materials centers, professional libraries, and curriculum materials laboratories, basically, is the professional staff of the school system. Included are the staff of individual schools—teachers, counselors, librarians, and principals—and the professional staffs of the various central-office departments.

Related to clientele magnitude is the number of schools in the school system, which provides further indication of the extent to which central-office library services must be provided. The number of schools to which the materials center circulates materials and equipment should, therefore, be reported.

Pupils are the ultimate clientele for certain types of materials (such as audio-visual materials) circulated from school-system materials centers. However, since pupils usually do not borrow directly from materials centers, it is recommended that they not be reported as part of the center's clientele.

Physical Facilities. It is recommended that data concerning physical facilities for school-system materials centers not be collected on a regular basis, although this would be a suitable subject for special studies. Since many of the services of materials centers do not involve direct services to their clientele in a library situation, but rather the sending of material to schools for redistribution, questions concerning seating capacity would not be pertinent, except for professional libraries which maintain a reading room for teacher use. Most of the area of a central materials center is made up of work space, storage areas for different types of equipment and materials, materials production areas, and office space.

Collections. The collections in school-system central offices are usually different from those in school libraries, with greater emphasis on audio-visual materials. Book and periodical collections more frequently consist of material for teachers rather than for pupils. A statistical program should provide for reporting each type of material of importance, as follows:

Audio-visual materials:
  Films
  Filmstrips
  Recordings
  Other audio-visual materials

Printed materials:
  Professional books
  Textbooks
  Other books (including children's books)
  Professional periodicals
  Other printed materials

Other materials and audio-visual equipment lent to schools:
  Museum objects and realia
  Exhibits
  Audio-visual equipment

The information for school-system central office collections should be reported for:

The number of items at the beginning of the reporting period
The number of items added during the reporting period
The number of items withdrawn during the reporting period
The number of items at the end of the reporting period

For periodicals, however, the number of subscriptions currently received and the number of back volumes (bibliographic volumes) should be reported. Books should be reported by volume, and other materials by the appropriate unit of measurement—reel, disc, etc.

Services. The types of service offered by school-system materials centers should be reported by means of a checklist, and should include the following services:

> Maintains a collection of professional materials
> Maintains a sample textbook collection
> Maintains a collection of materials for review by teachers and
> librarians
> Circulates films to schools
> Circulates filmstrips to schools
> Circulates recordings to schools
> Circulates collections of books to schools
> Circulates audio-visual materials to schools
> Produces instructional materials for school use
> Provides other services (specify)

Personnel. Both professional and non-professional personnel assigned to school-system materials centers should be reported, with part-time employees reported in full-time equivalents. Professional personnel should be subdivided to show the number of librarians and the number of audio-visual specialists. Since most nonprofessional employees will be assigned to clerical tasks, no subdivision is needed.

Staff salaries for the central-office materials center should be reported in the same brackets recommended for school library staff. Report 10-, 11-, and 12-month salaries separately. The following personnel categories are recommended:

> Director (Head librarian)
> Assistant librarians
> Audio-visual specialists

When central-office professional personnel serve in more than one capacity, report their salaries under the position of their major assignment.

Expenditures. Expenditures for school-system materials centers should be reported under the following categories:

Operating Expenditures
    Salaries of materials center staff:
        Salaries of professional personnel
        Salaries of nonprofessional personnel
    Expenditure for books:
        Professional books
        Textbooks
        Other books
    Expenditures for periodicals and newspapers
    Expenditures for audio-visual materials
    Expenditures for binding and rebinding
    Expenditures for maintenance of equipment
    Expenditures for film rental
    Other expenditures, such as supplies, etc.
Capital Expenditures
    Expenditures for audio-visual equipment
    Expenditures for other equipment
    Expenditures for the initial collection of materials, or for a
    major expansion of the materials collection

School-Library Supervision

Rapid and continuing development of school-library supervision in local school systems has created a need for statistical information concerning this activity.

Personnel. Both school library supervisors and their clerical staffs should be reported. Personnel devoting less than full time to school library supervision should be reported in full-time equivalency. Personnel who serve in more than one capacity in school-system central office services for school libraries should be indicated by appropriate fractions in each category. Librarians assigned to the school-system central office who serve as part-time librarians in two or more schools should be reported by the school rather than the central office.

School library supervisors should be reported as follows:

Number of school library supervisors serving elementary schools only

Number of school library supervisors serving secondary schools only

Number of school library supervisors serving all schools in school system

Number of school library supervisors serving all schools in a geographical subdivision of the school system

Personnel who have the responsibility of supervising school libraries and librarians should be reported as professional personnel, including those with titles, such as director, coordinator, consultant, advisor, specialist, head librarian, or other titles used in local school systems.

Under nonprofessional personnel, only those clerical workers serving school library supervisors should be reported, with part-time employees reported in full-time equivalents.

Salaries of school library supervisors should be reported in the same way as salaries in school libraries, using the following categories:

Head school-library supervisor
Assistant school-library supervisors

Staff and Schools Supervised. The number of school librarians and the number of school libraries supervised by each school library supervisor is useful to determine the supervisor's work load. It is recommended that the number of school librarians and the number of school libraries supervised be reported by level of school, using three categories: elementary schools, secondary schools, and combined elementary-secondary schools.

Expenditures. The four chief types of expenditures for school library supervision are salaries, transportation and travel, instructional expenses, and supplies. Materials used by supervisors are likely to be from school-system materials centers and will be reported by the centers, or from an office collection, which should not be reported at all.

Salaries should be reported in two categories:

Supervisors' salaries
Clerical salaries

If supervisors serve part time in other services, such as school-system materials centers, only the appropriate fraction of the full salary should be reported here.

Instructional expenses include funds for in-service education programs, publications issued by the supervisor, and other expenses directly related to the supervising function.

Services. Services provided or coordinated by school library supervisors are varied and often are performed to a greater or lesser degree, requiring evaluation as well as enumeration. Comprehensive treatment of services of school library supervisors can be more effectively surveyed in special studies. It is recommended that they not be included in regularly recurring statistics.

School-System Central Processing Centers

The third major element in school-system central office services for school libraries is centralized ordering, cataloging, and processing of materials. The most significant information concerning central processing centers relates to personnel, libraries served, expenditures, and services.

Libraries Served. The libraries served by the school-system processing center should be reported by checklist using the following categories:

All schools in the system
Elementary schools only
Secondary schools only
New schools only
School-system materials center

Services. Both the types of service provided, and the output of central processing centers, should be reported.

Types of service should be indicated by a checklist including the following categories:

Centralized ordering of materials
Centralized cataloging of materials
Physical preparation of materials

Output should be reported by number of items processed for schools and for school-system materials centers, subdivided by type of material, as follows:

Number of books
Number of films
Number of filmstrips
Number of recordings
Number of other materials

Personnel. Both professional and nonprofessional personnel should be reported, using full-time equivalents for part-time personnel and for personnel with divided assignments.

Salaries of the professional staff in school-system central processing centers should be reported in the same manner as salaries in school libraries, using the following categories:

Director of processing center
Assistant librarians

Expenditures. Expenditures for central processing centers are of interest in determining the costs of acquisitions, cataloging, and processing of materials. The following items of expenditure should be reported:

Operating Expenditures
  Salaries:
    Salaries of professional personnel
    Salaries of nonprofessional personnel
  Bibliographies and other aids used in technical processing
  Expenditures for supplies
  Other expenditures
Capital Expenditures
  Equipment

Salaries of personnel who devote only part time to centralized processing should be reported as appropriate fractions of total salaries.

Intermediate Administrative Units

In this chapter, the discussion of the collection of basic school-library statistics has been limited to the primary units of school administration, namely, the school and the school system. Another unit—the intermediate administrative unit—does exist in many states, generally at the county level and primarily to provide consultative, advisory, or statistical services to the local units. In connection with the provision of services, the intermediate units (mainly in California) maintain "county-schools libraries," which provide library materials and services to contracting schools in much the same fashion as a school-system materials center.

VI

Statistics of

Special Libraries

The problems involved in measuring the characteristics of special libraries may be traced to the starting point of this Project, namely, the definition of *library*. To this end, the traditional definitions of *library* (including that in the A.L.A. *Glossary of Library Terms*) have been reconsidered and a general definition has been provided which embraces *collection, staff services,* and *clientele* as concepts without which no library exists (see glossary). We have also defined a special library as a type of library administered by and in behalf of an organized group which may be a business firm; a professional, scientific, or trade association; or a government, a hospital, or other nonprofit institution.

We now have two questions which confront us—(1) can we devise a set of criteria which will identify special libraries as a group, and (2) if this is possible, can we isolate homogeneous groups of special libraries for which meaningful comparative data can be collected?

Addressing ourselves to the first question, we note that a clear-cut distinction on the basis of sponsorship cannot be made. The sponsorship of a special library may be profit-making or nonprofit, or in industry, government, or services, resulting in an overlap with all other types of libraries. Since special libraries are spread across all fields of endeavor, the diversity of subjects and materials handled by the members of this class of libraries would preclude the establishment of a unique criterion based on subject-matter coverage. The same argument may also be advanced with respect to variation in services. Perhaps the only solution is to set up the requirement that a library which meets *all of the criteria* can be characterized as a special library. These criteria are:

1 The library's primary purpose is to supply information to its clientele, rather than to provide literature support for an educational program or to provide general materials for recreational reading.
2 Generally, the library is part of a larger organization whose major objectives are separate from but assisted by the provision of library services.
3 The services of the library are determined by the objectives of the sponsor, and the collection of the library is delimited by the subject areas of particular interest of the sponsor.
4 The librarian and his staff function as *primary* users of the library by interpreting the body of literature in the collection for the clientele.

In connection with the second question, the stratification of special libraries into homogeneous groups for purposes of statistical analysis will depend primarily on the collection of basic statistics. Only after a body of knowledge concerning these libraries has been developed can a scientific grouping be made. At the present time, only fragmentary statistical information is available concerning special libraries. However, the sobering necessity for finding solutions to problems (e.g., access to materials, education and recruitment as factors in expanding the numbers of trained personnel, the exploration of new techniques) has encouraged acceptance of the view that statistical measurements can be devised for special libraries.

For the purpose of statistical reporting, special subject departments of public libraries are to be reported as public libraries; departmental or specialized-school libraries of colleges and universities (e.g., the Baker Library of the School of Business, Harvard University; the Engineering Department Library, University of Michigan) are to be reported as college and university libraries; libraries administered by public school systems which provide professional materials to teachers and other members of the instructional staff are to be reported as a separate group under school libraries; specialized libraries serving state agencies and administered by the state library agency are to be reported with state library agency statistics.

There is another group of libraries which should not be considered special libraries although their sponsorship would lead one to believe they should be, for example, libraries serving personnel of army posts and naval stations, libraries for hospital patients, libraries serving federal institutions of higher education such as the Air University and Howard University, libraries serving elementary and secondary schools on military posts, etc.

The measurements needed to describe and evaluate special libraries will be the subject of this chapter.

Identification

In order to identify and describe the reporting library the following questions should be asked:

1 Name of library _____
2 Address _____
3 Organization _____
                             (name of institution, company, agency, or association which maintains this library)
4 How is this organization classified according to the Standard Industrial Classification (SIC)? _____
5 How is your library classified according to SIC, if it varies from that of the organization in which located? _____
6 Year library founded _____
7 Number of branches _____
8 Names and locations of other libraries in the establishment, if any _____
9 Year for which statistics are reported _____

The question arises as to the method of reporting the several libraries serving the employees of a single sponsor. One usually finds that major divisions of an industrial establishment have sufficiently individualized functions that the libraries attached to them are operating as independent libraries. *Each of these libraries should be reported separately.*

There are also instances in which the several libraries of an establishment have the characteristics of a single system containing a "central library" and one or more "branches," which may or may not be in locations different from that of the central library. *A single report should be submitted for such a "system" of libraries.*

The principal features which tend to identify a system of this type are:

All of the libraries are administered by a single library director.

The central library is larger and stronger, whereas the branches are smaller and more dependent.

Acquisition and cataloging are handled centrally.

There may, however, be situations in which only one or two of these features are observed, or the features are contradictory. Clearly, a fairly arbitrary stand has to be taken to ensure consistency of reporting. It is suggested that the *direction* of a library is the feature which most clearly establishes its character and hence its identity. If several libraries are secondary to a central library administered by a single library director, these should be reported as a system, whether the libraries are fully or partly centralized. If the system is decentralized to the point that each library has its own library director, these libraries will assume the character of independent libraries and in effect no system exists even if certain functions are performed centrally for all the libraries. These libraries should be reported as individual libraries even though the library directors themselves report to the same nonlibrary administrator.

For control purposes, a question should be included to determine the names and locations of all libraries within the organization.

The reporting period may be the calendar year or other fiscal year as used within the establishment. For comparability, all reports should be tabulated together for fiscal years in which a given January falls.

The date of a library's founding is not significant in relation to strength of collection, size of staff, or other variables. It should be asked, however, in order to provide data for tracing the growth of special libraries in the United States.

The use of the SIC will scatter the libraries more widely than the categories used in past library surveys (Personnel Survey, S.L.A. Standards Survey) but will facilitate standard reporting and comparability of data.

Population Served; Area of Service

The *population served* and *area of service* are concepts which are intended to determine the total population which may have access to libraries and their resources. For special libraries, service area as a geographic limitation is without importance. In order to determine the extent to which special libraries are providing and extending services, it is recommended that the following questions be directed to all special libraries:

1 What is the total number of employees of the sponsoring organization?

2 Of this number, how many employees are there to whom the services of the library are available?

The existence of a division library serving part of an organization to which a larger library provides organization-wide service can improve the service rendered but cannot extend the population served. In order to avoid duplicate reporting of population served, data on reports should be adjusted in order that population served by all libraries of the establishment does not exceed its total number of employees. Then, the sum of individual figures reported for employees served in any single class will give a *total number of employees in establishments served by special libraries, according to industry.*

Clientele

Determination of *clientele,* the persons actually using the library, poses important problems. Although it is widely agreed that the *size of clientele* is a significant figure in management analysis it must also be recognized that this measure is only one of a complex of factors in the audience potential of a special library. To obtain an actual count would necessitate complicated record-keeping tantamount to registration. Moreover, the size of clientele of one special library cannot be effectively compared with that of another special library differing from the first in mission and in provision of services. The size of clientele can be compared only with itself, that is, in terms of growth or diminution from year to year. Such growth is a useful internal measurement which libraries are urged to record as an aid in computing space requirements and planning services. However, such statistics have virtually no national significance. It is recommended that they not be collected for purposes of national reporting.

Hours of Service

It may be assumed that the special library providing services to the employees of an organization will maintain hours of service which match the organization's normal work week. Questions as to extended schedules or evening and week-end hours undertaken in order to provide for readers who are not able to use the library at other times are irrelevant for those establishments in which the usual commercial work week of forty to forty-eight hours is the prevailing pattern. Hours of service may affect library performance standards in hospitals where professional employees are required to be on duty around the clock. It is likely that the practice of leaving the library premises unlocked or allowing keys to users upon request is widespread, and questions as to hours of service will yield little information of value, except when undertaken as part of a special study in depth of a limited group of libraries.

Physical Facilities

Space and its allocation in special libraries is of continuing interest. Librarians often have to justify space estimates which, to nonlibrary administrators unfamiliar with the requirements of book trucks, public service desks, or periodical display shelves, seem unnecessarily large. Prominent consideration is being given at the present time to the development of standards for adequate space in special libraries. Statistics will be needed in order to develop and fortify these standards and will probably assume even greater importance in the future as growth of collections and services taxes existing facilities.

In a special library, a branch usually represents a subdivision of the library, placed for the convenience of certain clientele in a location apart from the central library. Functionally, it extends library services to a special type of clientele, rather than duplicates services. The data on the physical facilities of branches, therefore, should be added to that of the central library for an accurate measurement of the library facility.

The following items are recommended:

1 Total gross square feet of floor space _____
2 Seating capacity in reader area _____
   meeting rooms/conference areas _____
3 Volume capacity of the library _____
4 Total number of drawers in vertical files (letter or legal size) _____

Detailed information concerning specific areas, such as reader area, work area, stack area, storage area, meeting rooms and conference areas, etc., may be obtained by special study.

Collections

The fundamental purpose in reporting statistics of collections is to establish what portion of the nation's total book, periodical, and other library-material holdings exist in special libraries. An accurate count of the number of volumes is one of the most difficult statistics for many libraries to produce, particularly those with small staffs and informal procedures. Yet, a true count of these collections is necessary for statistical validity, and it is recommended that procedures necessary to accurate reporting be established.

In special libraries, the book stock and periodicals collection should be reported as separate totals. The very great reliance upon the most up-to-date material for current information results in the stressing of periodical literature and a particular awareness of the adequacy of the periodicals collection.

Book Stock. The physical volume is recommended as the basic unit for reporting the total book collection (see glossary). The choice of the physical volume in preference to the book title as a unit for counting is based upon the assumption that the bulk of book stock is received in the library already in bound form. Hence, the volume count is comparable from one library to another; whereas the title count, being subject to variation because of differing cataloging practices, would be less comparable.

Several problems, however, are recognized:

Varying binding practices may cause a collection of pamphlets, individually cataloged, to be reported as one volume in one library and several volumes in another library.

The existence of duplicate copies will elevate the volume figure without adding to the bibliographic strength of the collection.

Neither of these difficulties is of sufficient magnitude to justify a complete count by titles either as a substitute for the volume count or as an additional method undertaken as a check on the volume count. A check on the current volume-to-title ratio may be made by computing the *ratio of volumes added to the number of titles added during the reporting year.*

In special libraries, the existence of a moderate number of duplicate copies may be viewed as strengthening the collection. These libraries do not generally have the degree of duplication found in a public or academic library system. In certain institutions, such as hospitals, the possible existence of a teaching program should be considered, and queried accordingly, so that in comparing figures reported for collections, libraries supporting teaching programs may be distinguished from those without such programs.

Each library should be asked to report the *total number of volumes of book stock on hand at the beginning of the year, the number of volumes added, the number withdrawn,* and the *total number at the end of the year.*

Most libraries can, without difficulty, report the number of volumes added and the number withdrawn during the current year. In reports of the total collections of these same libraries a tendency to approximation is observed. Thus, for example, we may see the following figures reported:

Number of volumes of book stock at beginning of year 15,000
Number of volumes of book stock added during year   247
Number of volumes of book stock withdrawn during year   39

The question arises as to the accuracy of the figures 15,208 computed for the total book stock count at the end of the year. If the initial figure was an approximation, nothing other than further approximations can result no matter how accurately current figures are maintained.

It is suggested that each library first establish its procedures for counting book stock and periodical volumes added and withdrawn from the collection. Books purchased from nonlibrary funds for office or laboratory collections should not be reported.

If an accurate count of the total holdings has not been made in the past five years, such a count should be undertaken. If an immediate total count is impossible then it should be scheduled sequentially, one-fourth of the collection being counted each year (or even a smaller fraction, if necessary) until the count is finished. The initial approximation may be accepted as the base figure until the count has been completed.

Periodicals and Other Serials. Periodicals collections will include, in addition to periodicals and newspapers, those other serials such as annuals, memoirs, proceedings, and transactions which are treated in the same manner as periodicals. Two kinds of measurement are needed: (1) the total number of volumes in the periodicals collection, and (2) the extent of the periodicals collecting function, i.e., the number of titles currently received and the length of time these titles are retained.

The bibliographic volume (the volume assigned by the publisher) is recommended as the basic unit for reporting the periodicals collection. The physical volume, recommended for counting book stock, is a less reliable unit for periodicals, which are generally received prior to binding and may be assembled in various ways depending upon local binding practices. Greater comparability will result from one library to another if the volume assigned by the publisher is standardized as the basic unit. Extensive runs of periodicals which are retained in unbound form may be counted in like fashion and added to the total.

It is recognized that a reporting of physical volume counts would be desirable for computing space requirements for collections, but it is hoped that enough of this information can be obtained by special study to fulfill the needs of library administrators. For nationwide reporting, however, preference should be given to those measurements which provide the most information about periodicals collections as elements of total library resources.

With respect to the total periodicals collection, each library should be asked to report *the total number of volumes of periodicals on hand at the beginning of the year, the number of volumes added, the number withdrawn,* and *the total number at the end of the year.*

To measure the extent of the periodicals collecting function, each library should be asked the following:

1 Report the number of periodical titles currently received, exclusive of duplicate copies, according to whether these are received by purchase, by gift, or through exchange.

   By purchase (subscription or membership) _____

   By gift _____

   Through exchange _____

2 Indicate the number of titles which are retained in full in back files for the specified periods of time, according to whether these are full size or microform.

	Full size	Microform
At least 1 but not more than 5 years (includes new subscriptions intended to be retained 5 years)	_____	_____
More than 5 years but not indefinitely	_____	_____
Indefinitely	_____	_____

NOTE. Titles which have ceased publication and are no longer received by the library are to be included in each category as pertinent.

Nonbook Materials. The basic book stock and periodicals collection account for much, but not all, of the strength of special library holdings. In the third category, nonbook materials, a variety of other forms of publication deserves consideration. The reporting of these generally may be geared to the emphasis which the library places upon them, as will be discussed under "Special Collections," p. 105. Certain special considerations are briefly mentioned here because they affect the reporting of technical reports, audio-visual materials, and microform.

Technical Reports. It is recommended that the technical report be counted as a distinct major category in special libraries, *not as a part of the book collection.* This refers both to the internally-generated report, i.e., that published by the library's own sponsoring organization, and to the external report, acquired from outside the organization. Many libraries catalog, classify, and shelve their reports; and these reports meet the definition of a volume. Other libraries file reports with minimal or no cataloging, or separate their subject analysis from that of the book collection.

The extent of technical-report holdings in special libraries is of interest. Their unique bibliographic nature and the special considerations involved in their acquisition, retention, and circulation argue for reporting the number of technical reports in a separate category, whatever the library's method of handling them may be.

Audio-Visual Materials. Films, filmstrips, slides, and recordings (discs or tapes) are of importance in some special libraries. Filmstrips and slides should be counted by the piece. Motion picture film should be counted by the reel as stored in the library. Sound recordings on discs or tapes should also be counted by the physical unit. Because of the highly selective subject areas in which these holdings will constitute important collections, it is recommended that no count of titles be required for national reporting.

Microform. Questions about the collection of microform as an increasingly important form of publication in special libraries need to be formulated along two lines of inquiry:

1 To what extent do present-day collections exist in microform rather than as full-size materials?

This requires a collateral question supplementing each of those directed at determining the number of volumes added and withdrawn and the total number of volumes in the collections. The units used in each case would be the same as those used for full-size materials, i.e., the physical volume for books, the bibliographic volume for periodicals, and the individual report for technical reports (see "Collections" table, p. 106. It would not be necessary to indicate whether the form is microfilm, microcard, or microfiche.

In addition, the following question should be asked:

2 How much microfilm does the library have in its collection? How many microcards? How much microfiche?

Counting according to physical item is recommended in order to answer these questions. Microfilm should be counted by reel, the other forms by card or sheet.

The table summarizes the questions relating to the collections, as recommended in this section.

Special Collections. Still left to be counted are important holdings in forms that vary widely according to the special areas served. Some of the forms are rarely if ever found in other types of libraries (e.g., market surveys, advertising brochures); others are usually confidential within the sponsoring organization and hence unavailable except to the primary clientele (e.g., laboratory notebooks, correspondence files). They are not, however, incidental to the library's holdings, but essential components of the information resources.

Depending upon the emphasis which individual libraries place upon them, these unique materials may be retained as collections of like forms or they may be mingled, regardless of form, in general information files. If they are maintained as collections, they are resources having importance even beyond the individual li-

Collections

	Full-Size Material				Microform‖			
	Total beginning of year	No. added	No. withdrawn	Total end of year	Total beginning of year	No. added	No. withdrawn	Total end of year
Book Stock: Volumes*	⎯⎯	⎯⎯	⎯⎯	⎯⎯	⎯⎯	⎯⎯	⎯⎯	⎯⎯
Titles	XXX	⎯⎯	XXX	XXX	XXX	⎯⎯	XXX	XXX
Periodicals Collection†	⎯⎯	⎯⎯	⎯⎯	⎯⎯	⎯⎯	⎯⎯	⎯⎯	⎯⎯
Technical Reports:‡ Internal	⎯⎯	⎯⎯	⎯⎯	⎯⎯	⎯⎯	⎯⎯	⎯⎯	⎯⎯
External	⎯⎯	⎯⎯	⎯⎯	⎯⎯	⎯⎯	⎯⎯	⎯⎯	⎯⎯
Audio-Visual Materials:§								
Films	⎯⎯	⎯⎯	⎯⎯	⎯⎯	XXX	XXX	XXX	XXX
Filmstrips	⎯⎯	⎯⎯	⎯⎯	⎯⎯	XXX	XXX	XXX	XXX
Slides	⎯⎯	⎯⎯	⎯⎯	⎯⎯	XXX	XXX	XXX	XXX
Recordings (discs and tapes)	⎯⎯	⎯⎯	⎯⎯	⎯⎯	XXX	XXX	XXX	XXX
Other_____	⎯⎯	⎯⎯	⎯⎯	⎯⎯	XXX	XXX	XXX	XXX

*Count according to definition of *volume* (see glossary).
†Count according to definition of *bibliographic volume* (see glossary).
‡Count by individual report.
§Count by physical item (reel, slide, strip, disc, tape).
‖Count as the original material would be counted.

brary. It is assumed that the availability of these collections of nonbook materials can be readily indicated by the special library. The following question is recommended:

Specify by a check which of the following nonbook materials is maintained by your library as a special collection:

_____ Advertising brochures

_____ Annual reports (firms, institutions, societies)

_____ Clippings (newspaper)

_____ Legislative materials

_____ Maps

_____ Patents

_____ Research and laboratory notebooks

_____ Sheet music

_____ Trade catalogs

Other (specify)

_____   _____

_____   _____

NOTE. Collections containing fewer than 100 items should not be reported—see "Miscellaneous File Materials" below.

Miscellaneous File Materials. Libraries which do not maintain nonbook materials in special collections may collect them in general information files. The quantities of materials in such files should be reported in number of linear feet, thus rendering comparable those files which are retained in cabinets and those which are shelved.

Circulation

Traditionally the circulation function encompasses those activities of a library directed toward making materials from its collections available by loan to its clientele. In special libraries, the function should be thought of in terms of dissemination of information, rather than exclusively the loan of materials. It seems advisable to consider as part of the circulation function all those activities relating to (1) the loan of materials from the library's own collection, (2) interlibrary loan—either borrowing or lending, and (3) provision of photocopies in lieu of lending materials.

Circulation figures admittedly give an inadequate picture of the use of the collection because they do not show the use of materials in the library; still, circulation is a phase of the output of information and its volume should be counted. Special libraries should be asked to report the circulation of technical reports in addition to books, periodicals, and audio-visual materials.

Circulation between libraries which are administratively independent, though in departments or locations of the same establishment, should be reported as interlibrary loans. Materials made available to branches, or by branches to central libraries, should be counted only as loans to borrowers, not as interlibrary loans.

The number of photocopies supplied in lieu of materials lent to clientele or to other libraries should also be reported. The table summarizes the information which should be reported.

	Circulation		
	No. Items	*Interlibrary Loans†*	
	Lent*	*Lent*	*Borrowed*
Book Stock			
Periodicals			
Technical Reports			
Audio-Visual Materials			
Photocopies supplied in lieu of materials‡			

*Excluding interlibrary loans.
†Excluding loans between central library and branches or between individual branches.
‡In counting photocopy reproductions, count a reproduction of a book or part of a book as a single item. Similarly, a pamphlet, report, patent, or thesis, or part of any of these, should be counted as a single item. Photocopy reproductions prepared from periodical material, however, should be counted in terms of the number of articles copied, a full article or part of an article being counted as a single item.

It is also recommended that questions be added which will determine the extent to which routine circulation adds to requested circulation.

1 Does the library circulate new journals to clientele by means of routing lists? _____ Yes _____ No

2 If "Yes," how many journals (titles) receive routine circulation? _____

Reference and Bibliographic Services

Reference and bibliographic services in special libraries include those activities undertaken in anticipation of user demand as well as those undertaken in response to specific requests. These activities include abstracting, reference work, bibliography compilation, literature searching, and research. Legislative-history compilation and reviewing may functionally also be classed in this area.

The reporting of the number of reference questions handled is recommended as a recurring statistic, but only as an indication of the size of the operation. It tells little about the scope of the service rendered and should be supplemented by more detailed studies at intervals, possibly on a sampling basis. These would be directed toward a level of detail which would make qualitative analysis of the service closer to realization.

Bibliographic services performed in libraries should be reported as number of items abstracted and number of items indexed according to type of material (internal reports, other technical reports, periodical articles, patents, legislative materials, etc.). Translations prepared by the library and translations obtained from outside sources should also be reported according to type of material translated (monographic material, abstracts, periodical articles, patents, correspondence, etc.). The questions in the table might be asked of those libraries which perform such services.

Another trend of prospective importance is the growth in contracted reference and bibliographic services. Because of the possibility of double-reporting it is recommended that two general questions be included to determine whether or not such contractual services are in operation. Any inquiries about numbers of items handled in each category of service should be reserved for follow-up study.

Bibliographic Services

1 If the library regularly indexes and/or abstracts periodical articles, reports, patents, etc., indicate in the columns below how many documents are handled in each service:

	Number of Documents	
	Indexed	*Abstracted*
Internal reports		
Other technical reports		
Periodical articles		
Patents		
Legislative materials		
Other (specify)		
Total		

2 If the library prepares translations or obtains them from commercial sources, translation pools, etc., indicate in the spaces provided how many documents are translated and the number obtained from outside sources according to type of document:

	No. documents translated	*No. translations obtained from outside sources*
Monographic material (count as one item all selections from one monograph)		
Abstracts		
Periodical articles		
Patents		
Correspondence		
Other (specify)		
Total		

The following questions should be directed to all special libraries:

1 Does the library obtain reference or bibliographic services upon contract from an outside agency or another library (e.g., literature searching, indexing, abstracting)? _____ Yes _____ No

2 Does the library supply reference or bibliographic services upon contract to other institutions (including other libraries)? _____ Yes _____ No

Technical Services

Almost all of the data which can be reported under acquisition, cataloging, classification, binding, and other areas of technical services are primarily work-load figures used for purposes of internal control. Statistical coordination in this area, therefore, is essentially a matter of uniform definitions. Statistics on the number of items acquired have been treated in the section on "Collections," p. 106, and expenditures in the section on "Expenditures," p. 114. It is recommended that no further detail be requested under this heading.

It is recognized, however, that reliable data on basic trends in technical services may prove to be of long-term significance. As a special study, it is recommended that special libraries be asked questions on the activity of the library in the purchase of catalog cards and precataloged books, the operation of its own bindery, and the use of a published classification system.

Personnel

The number of positions in special libraries and the salaries paid in each class are of general interest and usefulness. It is proposed that questions be asked in the following categories in order to obtain needed statistics.

Number of Library Staff Positions. Determination of the number of library staff positions in special libraries requires a count of three elements: full-time filled positions, part-time filled positions, vacant positions. A full-time position is one that requires the incumbent to work the total work week of the library. Full-time equivalents of part-time positions should be determined by adding all the hours worked per week in all part-time positions within the desired category and dividing by the number of hours within the total work week of the library. When fractional positions result, any fraction up to one-half should be dropped, and any fraction one-half or over should be rounded to the next full number.

It is recommended that these data be requested in terms of positions rather than in terms of the incumbents of these positions, so as to improve comparability in reporting among special libraries. A position can be classified into one of the three areas with less bias than would exist if the qualifications of the incumbent of the position were considered.

The following table calls for number of full-time, part-time, and vacant positions according to whether these are professional-librarian, professional-other, or nonprofessional.

Number of Filled and Vacant Positions

	Professional		Nonprofessional
	Librarian	Other	
Number of full-time positions filled			
Number of part-time positions filled (in full-time equivalents)			
Total filled positions (in full-time equivalents)			
Number of vacant positions			

> NOTE. Maintenance positions should be excluded because they are not significant in the evaluation of the library program and because they are usually not included with the library staff roster.

Although the definition of "professional personnel" does not refer to the amount of academic background and statistics which would fully describe characteristics of library staff members would have to be the subject of a special study, the following question should be included:

> How many library school graduates holding a fifth-year degree in librarianship are on the staff? _____

Salaries of Full-Time Professional Staff Members. Because library staff salaries are usually considered confidential, it is not practical to ask for specific salaries paid to each staff member. While precise figures may not be obtainable, the salary brackets in the following table are detailed enough to be useful. Each library is requested to report the numbers of staff members in the salary brackets specified in the portion of the table appropriate for its own full-time professional staff complement.

Salaries of Full-Time Professional Staff

	Under $5,000	$ 5,000-$ 5,999	$ 6,000-$ 6,999	$ 7,000-$ 7,999	$ 8,000-$ 8,999	$ 9,000-$ 9,999	$10,000-$10,999	$11,000-$11,999	$12,000-$12,999	$13,000-$13,999	$14,000-$14,999	$15,000-$19,999	$20,000 and over
A. Libraries with 1-4 professional staff members:													
Library Director													
Other Professional Staff													
B. Libraries with 5 or more professional staff members:													
Library Director													
Assistant Director													
Department Head													
Assistant Department Head													
Other Professional Staff													

NOTE. The position of director of a special library should be classified as "professional-librarian" regardless of the training or experience of the incumbent of this position or the size of the library.

In addition, the following question should be asked:

What is the beginning salary the library offers for its lowest full-time professional staff position? $_____

Salaries reported here should be based on gross salary prior to deductions, but without bonuses, fully-paid pensions, health plans, or stock. The total number should agree with the total of full-time professional positions in the preceding table.

It is not intended that information be published in connection with any individual special library, but that summaries be used to illustrate trends in professional remuneration according to sponsorship, industry, size of professional staff, and area.

Income

The only figures relating to source of income which might be of interest are those which would indicate multiple sources of income. Special libraries as a class are sponsored by individual organizations. Their funds come from the sponsoring organizations. The type of sponsorship has been reported in response to an earlier question (i.e., "Standard Industrial Classification") and specific questions relating to funds can elicit no further information. Though it is possible that funds are received from sources other than the sponsoring organization, such as gifts, bequests, fees for services, etc., special libraries having such sources of income are believed to be a very small fraction of the total number. Consequently, it is recommended that no questions regarding sources of income be directed to special libraries.

Expenditures

Expenditures, except for buildings, can be reported according to categories which are comparable with those of other types of libraries. Because most special libraries do not own their own buildings, their capital expenditures will be limited to those for equipment. Expenditures for rent, debt service, or insurance would usually also be assumed by the sponsoring organization.

Figures reported should be actual expenditures, rather than budgeted figures. Expenditures for book stock, periodicals collection, and nonbook materials should be those for items purchased by the library and charged to library funds; items charged to funds of other departments should be excluded. However, it is considered impractical to exclude from the total expenditures for personnel that portion which was allocated to the acquisition (and possibly cataloging) of publications for departments; hence it is recommended that the figure for library personnel expenditures remain intact. Expenditures for part-time staff members who also work in other departments should include only that portion of the salaries prorated for time worked in the library.

The following list of questions is recommended for all special libraries to cover the necessary reporting of expenditures:

Operating Expenditures
Expenditures for personnel:
Library personnel (excluding maintenance
personnel) _____

Other personnel costs
(social security; retirement/pension)   _____
Total personnel costs   _____
Expenditures for library materials:
  Book stock   _____
  Periodicals collection   _____
  Audio-visual materials   _____
  Other nonbook materials   _____
  Total library materials costs   _____
Expenditures for binding and rebinding   _____
Supplies and other operating expenditures,
total to include:
  Stationery and supplies
  Printing and advertising
  Photocopying expenditures
  Postage, freight, express
  Repairing and mending
  Replacement of equipment
  Travel
  Memberships
  Other   _____
Total operating expenditures   _____

Capital Expenditures

All capital expenditures to include:
  New buildings and additions to existing
  buildings; major structural changes, with
  all architects' fees, permits, etc.
  Equipment for new or expanded buildings
  (including initial library materials);
  additional equipment for existing buildings.
Total capital expenditures   _____
Total expenditures, operating and capital   _____

Data Processing

The impact of the mechanization of information processing has been so great that we are now entering a new era of library service. Certainly the growth of data processing has brought a new group of specialists into the library personnel area, new techniques to be learned, and new effectiveness to the work of librarians. At the present time, the impact of the new technology can be measured more in its effect on traditional services of libraries than as a new service in itself. For that reason, we recommend the following questions as illustrative of those which might be asked to determine trends in this fast-developing area. It is probable that in the relatively near future the pattern of these activities will become clearer, and more specialized studies can be undertaken.

1 Acquisition
   Does the library use any mechanized system as part of its acquisition function? _____ Yes _____ No
2 Circulation
   Is any mechanized system used in printing routing lists? _____ Yes _____ No
   Is any mechanized system used in the circulation operations other than routing lists? _____ Yes _____ No
   If "Yes," specify: _____

The development of mechanized systems is of more interest in the area of reference and bibliographic services than in any other area of library service. The future will probably see a steady expansion in the number and complexity of mechanized information storage and retrieval systems.

Only the first of these two aspects needs to concern us here. Questions should be directed to all libraries in order to disclose the existence or absence of mechanized systems for reference and bibliographic work. All further inquiry with regard to the scope of these activities, types of equipment in operation, and performance details should be made the subject of a special study directed to those actually engaged in such activity. Recommendations for the reporting of numbers of reels of computer tapes or items in punched card files seem premature until such time as more is known about the general types of systems in which devices are utilized.

The following question should be directed to all special libraries:

3 Reference and Bibliographic Services
   Does the library use any mechanized system in its bibliographic work (indexing, searching, printing, bibliographies, etc.)? _____ Yes _____ No

VII

Statistics of

Library Education

In one of the Background Papers for the A.L.A. Conference Within a Conference held in Chicago in the summer of 1963, Charles M. Armstrong concluded: "The outstanding solid fact in the problem of staffing the libraries ... is that there will be a shortage of professionally-trained librarians. The shortage will be serious if their use is confined to the most urgent operations. If an attempt is made to continue past manning policies, the shortage may be crippling. In any case, available personnel is likely to be a limiting factor in the growth of the libraries and it should be carefully budgeted and conserved."[1]

The seriousness of the shortage of professional library personnel can be demonstrated variously. State librarians report that before they can expand public library programs they must recruit additional competent extension librarians. According to school library supervisors, scores of school librarians are needed to provide library service for rapidly expanding elementary and secondary school programs. Several hundred librarians are needed to develop materials and library-service programs for the new vocational and technical institutes. In special libraries there is heavy demand for subject specialists and for librarians with foreign language competency. Library schools, graduate and undergraduate, need additional able teachers.

There is important work to be done in strengthening the undergraduate and graduate library-education program, which is

---

[1] "Staffing Library Services to Meet Student Needs; Services and Personnel Management," p.7.

largely responsible for educating today's librarians. For purposes of comparison and for interpretation of library-education standards, much information is needed by library educators and practitioners who serve as either full- or part-time members of library-school faculties, on library-school advisory committees, and on library-school evaluation committees. The states which are undertaking statewide planning to recruit and educate in a responsible way for their library programs also need reliable data to assist them in their deliberations.

Library-school statistics are critically needed on a regular basis for enrollments, degrees, faculty, budget, and salaries. Also needed, from time to time, is information which can be obtained from special studies of curricula, summer session programs, the opportunities for continuing education, faculty work load (including committee assignments, direction of theses, research, etc.), faculty research and publication, tuition costs, admission policies, degree requirements, etc. Another means of providing useful information relative to effective training and utilization of library manpower would be a summarization of the follow-up studies that library schools make of their alumni. Such a survey would yield more useful information if there were some advance coordination and standardization of the instrument to be used by the individual school.

For the first major statistical survey in the field of library education, it is recommended that the universe include all institutions of higher education listed in the *USOE Education Directory. Part 3: Higher Education.*

Enrollment in Library Science

The enrollment statistics indicated below should be made available just as soon as possible after the final fall session registration period (registration generally completed by the third week in October). The data requested at this time would also include a second part requesting enrollment reports for the previous summer session and a third part requesting enrollment reports for the previous academic year.

Degrees Awarded in Library Science

For the academic year and for the summer session covered by a given survey, each library education program would report as indicated below the number of degrees according to sex of graduate and level of degree awarded. In the initial survey, at least,

Student Enrollment in Library Science

in institutions of higher education

Degree Level	No. enrolled full time			No. enrolled part time		
	Men	Women	Total	Men	Women	Total
Graduate:						
Master's						
Intermediate*						
Doctorate†						
Undergraduate‡						
Special students§						
Total						

*Include all post-Master's students who are not working toward a doctorate but toward the completion of an advanced, cohesive program of library education.

†Include only those in residence taking full- or part-time loads.

‡Include here students in prerequisite courses as well as undergraduates from the School of Education and from other schools or departments. Exclude students enrolled in "How to Use the Library" courses.

§Report here all students registered as special students, i.e., those not reported elsewhere in the table who are not candidates for degrees, such as those fulfilling nondegree certification requirements or taking courses as unclassified students.

Degrees in Library Science

number of degrees granted
by level of degree and sex of graduate

Degree	Number granted	
	Men	Women
Bachelor's*		
Master's†		
Second-level Master's‡		
Doctorate		
Other (specify) _____		
Total		

*Report here all four-year degrees awarded in library science.

†Report here all first Master's degrees in library science.

‡Report here all degrees which represent second Master's degrees in library science, sometimes called sixth-year Master's.

it would be desirable to ask for parallel information on degrees awarded by other academic units for library science majors.

Tuition Costs

An additional area of investigation, namely, the compilation of tuition costs in library schools, has been suggested as an important adjunct to a complete investigation of library education. We agree that a study of trends in tuition costs may be one of the primary factors affecting enrollment. However, it is recommended that such an investigation be conducted as a special study because of its complexity.

Placement of Graduates

Since 1955, reports on employment and earnings for the new fifth-year graduates of A.L.A. accredited library schools have appeared in each June 15 issue of the *Library Journal*.[2] Following are the major *Library Journal* placement categories:

Placement by Type of Library

Type of Library	Number of Known Placements
Public	
Municipal	
County and regional	
School	
College and university	
Special and other	
Total	

Library School Teaching Loads

A critical element in quality library-education is a competent faculty adequate in number to carry out educational objectives. The number of full-time and part-time faculty and an indication of their teaching loads provide useful information for purposes

---

[2]Prepared by Donald E. and Ruth B. Strout, e.g.: "The Word Is More," pp. 2451-57 (1963).

of comparison and evaluation. Credit-hour registration will also be used in calculating unit costs. Information requested for the fall and the previous summer session should include the following:

Library Science Courses
credit-hour registration

	Semester hours	Trimester hours	Quarter hours
Courses			
Undergraduate courses			
Graduate courses, excluding doctoral program			
Doctoral program			
Normal Full-Time Credit-Hour Load			
Per student:			
Undergraduate			
Graduate			
Per faculty member:			
Undergraduate			
Graduate			

Number of Library Science Faculty
by rank and teaching load

Rank	Total number	No. of hours taught (class contact hours)			Percent of work load devoted to teaching
		Semester	Trimester	Quarter	
Full-Time					
Professor					
Associate Prof.					
Assistant Prof.					
Instructor					
Other (specify) _____					
Part-Time					
Professor					
Associate Prof.					
Assistant Prof.					
Instructor					
Other (specify) _____					

In computing credit-hour registration, the level of the course is to determine the graduate or undergraduate level of the registration. Ten students registered in a 3-semester hour course would provide a total of 30 semester hours of registration. Students who audit courses or take noncredit courses should be excluded. For courses offered jointly by the library school and some other academic unit (e.g., the same course in children's literature might be listed in the catalog by both the library school and the school of education), only those students in courses actually taught by library science faculty should be counted.

In order to measure the total faculty work load, it is recommended that additional information be collected concerning non-teaching activities of faculty members, such as research, committee assignments, etc. The proportion of faculty time devoted to teaching at the graduate level should be studied when programs at both graduate and undergraduate levels are offered.

Income and Expenditures

According to the A.L.A. *Standards for Accreditation*, "The adequacy of the financial provision for a library school shall be judged in relation to the number of students, program of professional education, the financial support and salary schedule of the institution, and necessary instructional facilities and equipment." Similarly the A.L.A. budget standard for *Undergraduate Programs in Librarianship* is as follows: "An initial appropriation to secure equipment, instructional materials, and library facilities shall be made by the institution establishing a library science program. Thereafter, an annual budget adequate to support the program of instruction and to secure its continuing development shall be provided."

To provide meaningful data on financial support for library education, information on income and expenditures such as the categories noted below might be considered. Instructions should specify summer session and academic year to be reported, and should include the basis for estimating the monetary value of contributed services, e.g., teaching without compensation performed by members of religious orders, etc.

Income and Expenditures

1 Income
  Funds received from the institution for the
  library education program   _____

Contractual services _____

Grants or other special funds received for
the library education program _____

Other funds for use of the library education
program (specify) _____

Total Income _____

2 Operating expenditures (not capital expenditures)

Salaries (gross salaries) _____

Administration (prorate on basis of proportion of time spent on administration) _____

Instruction (include only compensation for
teaching) _____

Instruction assistance (e.g., revisers) _____

Research _____

Other (exclude maintenance; include library-
school librarian, secretaries, clerical assistants, etc.) _____

Fellowships and scholarships (exclude teaching assistantships reported under salaries) _____

Research projects or assistance to faculty for
research _____

Purchase of books _____

Lectures _____

Travel _____

Other (specify) _____

Total operating expenditures _____

3 Total expenditures of the institution for educational and general purposes _____

Salary Statistics

The shortage of professional librarians is reflected also in the
field of education for librarianship. The recruitment of competent library-school faculty members to replace those who are
retiring or otherwise leaving the profession, and to fill new
positions for expanding programs, is difficult at best. Deans of
schools which are not A.L.A. accredited schools or which do not
offer salaries competitive with the former find it next to impossible. The following table indicates the types of salary information needed. Two tables should be used to differentiate between

Salaries of Full-Time Staff Currently Employed

Exclude staff members employed on a part-time basis or for less than the
full academic year (minimum of 9 months)

Rank	Under $5,000	$5,000 to $5,999	(etc. by $1,000 steps to)	$19,000 to $19,999	$20,000 and over
Head of program					
Associate or assistant head of program					
Professor					
Associate Professor					
Assistant Professor					
Other instructional staff* (specify)					

*Include all other full-time members of the instructional staff not previously listed.

those faculty members employed on the basis of (a) 9-10
months and (b) 11-12 months.

Instructional Costs

Data should be secured on either a cost-per-student-hour
basis or a cost-per-student basis figured in full-time equivalents.
This will require information on total salary allocations for
library education for a specified fall session and the previous
summer session.

Instructional salaries are suggested as a means of studying
unit costs because adequate faculty is so important to quality
education and because library-education programs and institutional accounting practices vary so widely. If the instructions

are clear, it is possible to secure comparable data on instructional costs, as based upon instructional salaries and teaching load.

In Conclusion

One of the major concerns of every profession is maintaining programs of quality professional education. These programs must be successful in transmitting the knowledge, philosophy, ethics, and skills that constitute the discipline; promoting research and publication adequate to support sound graduate professional education; and providing practitioners with the intellectual and methodological resources requisite for meeting new demands intelligently, constructively, and creatively.

Librarians and library educators today are actively engaged in the task of strengthening library education—pre-service, in-service, and continuing. To plan effective programs for recruitment, library education, and library research, they must have up-to-date information of the type recommended in this chapter.

Terms Used in Statistical Surveys

This glossary contains definitions of terms used in this handbook. It is recommended that the glossary be referred to extensively while developing questionnaires for statistical surveys. The glossary is arranged alphabetically, with cross references where they are deemed necessary.

The sources from which the definitions have been taken are numerous, and it would be virtually impossible to provide a source citation for each definition because of the extensive editorial alterations that have been made. However, the principal source has been the *A.L.A. Glossary of Library Terms*, with such subsidiary sources as *The Common Core of State Educational Information* for school-library terms and the *Glossary of Terms Used in Special Libraries* for special-library terms.

ABSTRACT. A factual summary giving the significant content of a unit of publication (e.g., a scientific or scholarly paper, a technical report, a patent). It may accompany the full paper when originally published, or it may be issued separately with a citation referring to the original publication.

ABSTRACTING. The practice of summarizing a scientific or scholarly paper or report in order to render in brief form the essential factual content.

ACCREDITED LIBRARY SCHOOL. *See* LIBRARY SCHOOL, ACCREDITED.

ACQUISITION. The area of library service comprising the obtaining of books, periodicals, and other library materials by purchase, exchange, or gift, together with the maintenance of the necessary records of these additions.

ACQUISITIONS DEPARTMENT. The administrative unit in charge of acquiring books, periodicals, and other materials by purchase, exchange, or gift, and of keeping the necessary records of these additions. Sometimes referred to as Order Department or Accession Department.

ADMINISTRATION. (1) The active management of a library or library system. (2) The area of library service comprising the determination of policy and program, financial management, personnel coordination and supervision, and public relations for a library or library system.

ADULT EDUCATION. The acquisition of knowledge by those beyond school age through regularly organized programs which have as their purpose the development of skills, knowledge, habits, or attitudes.

ADVERTISING BROCHURES. Informational pamphlets issued by commercial firms as advertising for their products.

ADVISORY SERVICES. Counsel rendered to individuals, groups, organizations, institutions, libraries, and library systems, and to governmental bodies in the establishment, administration, and financing of library service and of library buildings and equipment. *See also* READERS' ADVISORY SERVICE.

AFFILIATED LIBRARY. A member of a library system. This library has its own board and is not administered by the central library, as is the case with a branch library.

ANNALS. *See* ANNUAL.

ANNOTATING. The practice of preparing notes that describe, explain, or evaluate publications entered in a bibliography, reading list, or catalog.

ANNOTATION. A note accompanying an entry in a bibliography, reading list, or catalog intended to describe, explain, or evaluate the publication referred to. A book annotation is called a book note. *See also* BIBLIOGRAPHY, ANNOTATED.

ANNUAL. A serial publication issued regularly once a year, as an annual report or proceedings of an organization; or, a yearly publication that reviews events or developments during a year, in descriptive and/or statistical form, sometimes limited to a special field. Also includes annals, yearbooks, etc.

ARCHIVES. The organized body of records made or received in connection with the transaction of its affairs by a government or a governmental agency, an institution, organization, or establishment, or a family or individual, and preserved for record purposes in its custody or that of its legal successors.

AREA OF SERVICE. A public library term applying to the geographical area and the residents thereof, to whom the library offers its services free of charge and from which (or on behalf of which) the library derives income.

ASSISTANT DEPARTMENT/DIVISION HEAD. Librarian ranking next to a Department/Division Head, having full-time duties as assistant to the Department Head and having responsibility for department activities in the absence of the Department Head.

ASSISTANT DIRECTOR. Librarian ranking next to the head of a library or library system, having full-time duties as the Director's assistant and having responsibility for library activities in the absence of the Director; may also be known as Associate Director or Deputy Director.

ASSISTANT LIBRARIAN. *See* ASSISTANT DIRECTOR.

ASSOCIATE LIBRARIAN. *See* ASSISTANT DIRECTOR.

ATTENDANCE, AVERAGE DAILY. In a given school year, the average daily attendance for a given school is the aggregate days attendance of the school divided by the number of days school was actually in session with pupils under the guidance and direction of teachers in the teaching process.

AUDIO-VISUAL AREA. An area in a library or serving as an adjunct to a library, designed or provided with special equipment for audio-visual materials storage, screening, and listening.

AUDIO-VISUAL MATERIALS. Nonbook library materials, such as recordings, transparencies, tapes, slides, films, and filmstrips, which require the use of special equipment in order to be seen or heard.

AUDIO-VISUAL SPECIALIST. A staff member of a library or school system engaged in activities related to the acquisition, use, and care of audio-visual equipment and to the techniques of presentation through the use of audio-visual equipment and materials.

AVERAGE DAILY ATTENDANCE. *See* ATTENDANCE, AVERAGE DAILY.

AVERAGE DAILY MEMBERSHIP. *See* MEMBERSHIP, AVERAGE DAILY.

BIBLIOGRAPHIC SERVICE. Those activities relating to the selection and dissemination of information from a specialized literature. These activities may be undertaken in anticipation of users' requests or in response to requests on a single or recurring basis.

BIBLIOGRAPHIC VOLUME. A unit of publication distinguished from other units by having its own title page, half title, cover title, or portfolio title. In connection with periodicals, the publisher's volume.

BIBLIOGRAPHY. A list of references to library materials organized for a particular use or relating to a particular subject.

BIBLIOGRAPHY, ANNOTATED. A bibliography which, in addition to identifying library materials, describes or evaluates their content and/or use with critical or explanatory notes.

BINDERY. An establishment that specializes in bookbinding.

BINDING AND REBINDING. The process of producing a single volume from leaves, sheets, signatures, or issues of periodicals, or of covering such a volume, either initially, as in the case of "binding," or as a thorough restoration of a volume, involving resewing and a new cover, as in the case of "rebinding." For statistical purposes, repairing and mending are not included with these activities.

BINDING OR BINDERY DEPARTMENT. The library department that prepares books, periodicals, and other library materials for binding outside the library. The activity may also include minor repair and mending.

BOARD OF DIRECTORS. A governing body of a library; also known as Library Board, Board of Trustees, and Library Trustees.

BOOK. A unit of publication, either bibliographically independent or a volume in a series published under the same title, consisting of leaves, sheets, or signatures sewn or otherwise bound together, covered or uncovered. Bound volumes of periodicals and newspapers are not considered books.

BOOK CAPACITY. *See* VOLUME CAPACITY.

BOOKLET. *See* PAMPHLET.

BOOKMOBILE. An automobile truck especially equipped to carry books and other library materials and serve as a traveling branch library.

BOOK NOTE. *See* ANNOTATION.

BOOK STOCK. A library's collection of books, or of other materials which are prepared and recorded in the same manner as books.

BRAILLE MATERIALS. Library materials for the visually handicapped using a system of embossed print.

BRANCH. (1) An auxiliary library with separate quarters, a permanent basic collection of books, a permanent staff, and a regular schedule, but administered from a central unit. (2) In college and university libraries, a branch consists of a special area or subject collection of library materials, serviced by its own staff. It is usually located on the same campus as the main library and is centrally administered.

BROADSIDE. A publication consisting of a single sheet printed on one side only, usually intended to be posted, publicly distributed, or sold.

BUDGET. An estimate of proposed expenditures for a given period or purpose and the proposed means of financing them.

BUILDING CONSULTANT. *See* ADVISORY SERVICES.

BULLETIN. A publication, usually numbered, issued at regular intervals by a government department, a society, or an institution.

CAPITAL EXPENDITURES. Expenditures which result in the acquisition of or addition to fixed assets, e.g., building sites, new buildings and building additions, equipment (including initial book stock), and furnishings for new or expanded buildings. Excludes investments for capital appreciation, and replacement and repair of existing furnishings and equipment.

CARD SERVICE. A serial publication which is revised, cumulated, and/or indexed by means of new or replacement cards which are filed in the library. It is used where latest revisions of information are important, as with scientific materials.

CARREL. An individual study area usually consisting of chair, table, and book shelf.

CATALOG. A list which records and describes the resources of a library. In a *card catalog,* unit entries are on separate cards, which are arranged in a definite order in drawers.

CATALOGED MATERIAL. Any library material which has been identified in a catalog which records, describes, and indexes the resources of a library; as distinct from library materials which are merely physically arranged for use and are not indexed and described individually by item.

CATALOGING, CENTRALIZED. *See* CENTRALIZED PROCESSING.

CENTRALIZED PROCESSING. The ordering of books, preparation of catalog records, and physical preparation of books in one library or a central agency for all libraries of a system (or area).

CENTRALIZED SCHOOL LIBRARY. *See* SCHOOL LIBRARY.

CENTRAL LIBRARY. The library which is the administrative center of a library system, where the principal collections are kept and handled. Also called Main Library.

CERTIFIED LIBRARIAN. *See* LIBRARIAN, CERTIFIED.

CHARTS. *See* NONBOOK MATERIALS.

CHIEF LIBRARIAN. *See* LIBRARY DIRECTOR.

CHILDREN'S DEPARTMENT. The administrative unit of a public library system that has charge of work with children in the central children's room and in all other agencies offering library service to children.

CIRCULATING LIBRARY. *See* TRAVELING LIBRARY.

CIRCULATION. The activity of a library in lending its resources to borrowers. For statistical purposes, photocopies provided in lieu of circulation should also be included.

CIRCULATION DEPARTMENT. (1) The part of a library from which books are lent for outside use. (2) The administrative unit in charge of all the routines connected with lending materials for outside use.

CLASSIFIED DOCUMENT. *See* REPORT, CLASSIFIED.

CLASSIFIED REPORT. *See* REPORT, CLASSIFIED.

CLASSROOM COLLECTION. (1) A semipermanent or a temporary collection of books deposited in a schoolroom by a public or a school library. (2) A group of books from a college library sent to a classroom for use by instructors and students.

CLERICAL PERSONNEL. *See* NONPROFESSIONAL PERSONNEL.

CLIENTELE. The persons actually using a library's services.

CLIPPING. An item of publication cut out of a newspaper or periodical.

COLLECTION. An accumulated group of library materials having a common characteristic, as Pamphlet Collection, Chemistry Collection, Mrs. Homer A. Fishheart Collection. (For a library's total holding, *see* LIBRARY COLLECTION.)

COLLEGE CATALOG. An official publication of a university or college giving regulations, announcements, information about curricula, courses, faculty, etc.

COLLEGE LIBRARY. (1) A library forming an integral part of a college, organized and administered to meet the needs of its students and faculty. (2) In a university library system, a library with a collection of books related to the work of a particular college and administered separately by the college or as a part of the university library.

COMBINED ELEMENTARY AND SECONDARY SCHOOL PLANT. *See* SCHOOL PLANT, COMBINED ELEMENTARY AND SECONDARY.

COMMUNITY SERVICES. Special services provided by a library for the community as a whole or for some segment of the community, e.g., lectures, concerts, book or art exhibits, discussion programs, and story hours.

CONSOLIDATED SYSTEM. A library system (*q.v.*) established by vote of several municipal governing bodies or by action of voters, and governed by the Board of Trustees of the system with individual units operating as branches of the system.

CONSULTANT, LIBRARY. *See* LIBRARY CONSULTANT.

CONSULTATIVE SERVICES. *See* ADVISORY SERVICES.

CONTRACT SERVICES. Items appearing in a library's statement of income representing funds received from a governmental, library, or other agency for specific services rendered, or in the statement of expenditures for services rendered to the library by individuals or agencies on the basis of a specific contract.

CONTRIBUTED SERVICES. Services in lieu of compensation, the cost of which is a part of normal overhead costs and the value of which can be estimated on the basis of 11-12 months of employment.

COOPERATING LIBRARY. A library that joins another library or group of libraries in some common plan, such as coordinated development of collections and services or contribution of entries to a union catalog.

COOPERATIVE SERVICES. The common services planned and coordinated by a cooperative system (*q.v.*).

COOPERATIVE SYSTEM. A group of independent and autonomous libraries banded together by informal or formal agreements or contracts which stipulate the common services to be planned and coordinated by the directors of the cooperative system.

COORDINATOR OF SCHOOL LIBRARIES. *See* SCHOOL LIBRARY SUPERVISOR.

COUNTY LIBRARY. A free public library service to county residents supported with county tax funds and administered as an independent agency or as part of another library agency.

COUNTY SCHOOLS LIBRARY. An instructional materials library maintained by the office of a county superintendent of schools providing materials and services to contracting schools.

CREDIT-HOUR REGISTRATION. The sum of the units used to measure course work undertaken by students in a given institution. One credit hour usually represents one hour of instruction per week in a given number of weeks.

CURRICULUM LABORATORY. A center which provides textbooks, curriculum guides, audio-visual materials, and other instructional materials for examination and study by teachers and other instructional staff of a school system.

CUSTODIAN. *See* MAINTENANCE PERSONNEL.

DEPARTMENT. (1) A major administrative unit of a library system set up to perform a definite function or set of related functions, and having its own staff and specified responsibilities, with a head directly responsible to the library director or to the assistant director. (2) A subject section in a library in which all books, periodicals, and other library materials, whether for reference or circulation, are separated according to subject into several divisions (as in some large public libraries); sometimes called Division.

DEPARTMENTAL LIBRARY. In colleges and universities, a special area or subject collection of library materials, possibly housed within the main library, and administratively linked to the branches. (For a library maintained by a Government Department, *see* GOVERNMENT LIBRARY.)

DEPARTMENT/DIVISION HEAD. The head of a major administrative unit of a library system or of a section devoted to a particular subject or group of subjects.

DEPOSIT LIBRARY. *See* STORAGE CENTER.

DEPOSITORY LIBRARY. *See* DOCUMENTS DEPOSITORY.

DEPOSIT STATION. A public library agency in a store, school, factory, club, or other organization or institution, with a small and frequently changed collection of books, and open at certain designated times. Also called Station.

DEPRECIATION ACCOUNT. An item occurring in a library's statement of expenditures which represents sums set aside for replacement of equipment. The amount of the sum is based upon the estimated lifetime of the equipment, e.g., a bookmobile.

DEPUTY DIRECTOR. *See* ASSISTANT DIRECTOR.

DEPUTY LIBRARIAN. *See* ASSISTANT DIRECTOR.

DIRECTOR. *See* LIBRARY DIRECTOR.

DIRECTOR OF SCHOOL LIBRARIES. *See* SCHOOL LIBRARY SUPERVISOR.

DIRECT SERVICE AREA. *See* AREA OF SERVICE.

DISCARD. To withdraw a book, periodical volume, or other item from the collection and from any records. *See also* WEEDING.

DISTRICT LIBRARY. *See* REGIONAL BRANCH.

DIVISION. *See* DEPARTMENT.

DIVISION LIBRARY. A collection attached to, and administered by, a division or a group of related departments of a university or a college, usually with some form of cooperative arrangement with the general library or as a part of the library system.

DOCUMENTATION. *See* BIBLIOGRAPHIC SERVICE.

DOCUMENT, GOVERNMENT. *See* GOVERNMENT DOCUMENT.

DOCUMENTS DEPOSITORY. A library legally designated to receive without charge copies of all or selected United States government publications; or a library designated to receive without charge a full set of Library of Congress printed cards.

EDITING. The practice of revising and preparing material for publication; it may be used in connection with library publications or with publications of the sponsoring organization originating outside the library.

ELEMENTARY SCHOOL. *See* SCHOOL, ELEMENTARY.

ENROLLMENT. (1) The total number of original entries in a given school unit. (2) For colleges and universities, the number of students enrolled full- and part-time on campus or in extension centers.

EPHEMERA. Material of transitory interest or value, consisting generally of pamphlets or clippings, which are usually kept for a limited time in vertical files.

EQUIPMENT. Items of a nonexpendable nature which retain their basic identity and utility over a period of time, as contrasted with supplies.

EXPENDITURES, CAPITAL. *See* CAPITAL EXPENDITURES.

EXPENDITURES, OPERATING. *See* OPERATING EXPENDITURES.

EXTENSION CENTER LIBRARY. A library branch located in a university or college extension center where college-level classes or other educational services are offered, usually through a specific division of an institution.

EXTENSION OF LIBRARY SERVICE. The promotion of libraries and of more extensive and intensive library services by national, state, regional, or local agencies; the supplying of books and other library assistance (including advisory services) to individuals and organizations outside a library's regular service area, and to areas in which library service is not otherwise available. *See also* ADVISORY SERVICES.

EXTENSION SERVICE. *See* EXTENSION OF LIBRARY SERVICES.

FACILITIES. A library's building (or quarters) and its equipment.

FEDERAL AID. *See* GRANT-IN-AID.

FEDERATED SYSTEM. A library system (*q.v.*) formed by joint action of governing bodies, but in which existing libraries continue to be governed by local boards; the central administration of the federated system coordinates and advises on cooperative services.

FIELD ADVISOR. *See* LIBRARY CONSULTANT.

FIELD VISIT. A direct, personal contact by a librarian or library consultant with a library agency, individual, group, organization, institution, or governmental body in the interest of stimulation, administration, or development of better library service. *See also* ADVISORY SERVICES; LIBRARY CONSULTANT.

FIELD WORK. *See* ADVISORY SERVICES; FIELD VISIT.

FILE. (1) Any equipment, such as vertical file, visible file, etc., in which records, cards, pamphlets, clippings, etc., are kept. (2) A collection of cards, pamphlets, clippings, etc., arranged systematically for reference.

FILMS. *See* AUDIO-VISUAL MATERIALS; NONBOOK MATERIALS.

FILMSTRIPS. *See* AUDIO-VISUAL MATERIALS; NONBOOK MATERIALS.

FISCAL PERIOD. Any period at the end of which a library or library system determines its financial condition and the results of its operations, and closes its books. NOTE. The period is usually a year, though not necessarily a calendar year.

FLOOR SPACE. The total area in the library devoted to library collections and services and to the working activities of the professional and nonprofessional staff. It includes work area, stack area, storage area, meeting rooms, and conference area, but not foyers, corridors, stairways, cafeterias, rest rooms, or heating plant area.

FOUR-YEAR HIGH SCHOOL. *See* SCHOOL, FOUR-YEAR HIGH.

FULL-TIME ENROLLMENT. Enrollment in not less than two-thirds of a full program (ten semester hours for a fifteen-semester-hour program; eight hours for a twelve-semester-hour program).

FULL-TIME EQUIVALENT. A fraction represented by time worked in a part-time position as the numerator and time required in a corresponding full-time position as the denominator.

FULL-TIME POSITION. A position the duties of which require the incumbent to be on the job the standard work week of the library, usually 35 to 40 hours. *See also* WORK WEEK.

GENERAL COLLECTION. That part of a library, particularly of a state library or of library functions at the state level, from which the primary readers' services emanate, as distinct from special collections and services for a particular clientele.

GENERAL LIBRARY. (1) A library not limited to a particular field or special subject. (2) The main library of a university library system. (3) That agency, performing library functions at the state level, which administers a state library's general collections.

GIFT AND EXCHANGE. The acquisition of library materials by gift, or in exchange with another library for publications of the library or its sponsoring body.

GOVERNMENT DOCUMENT. Any publication in book, serial, or nonbook form bearing a government imprint, e.g., the publications of federal, state, local, and foreign governments and of world organizations, such as United Nations, European Common Market, etc.

GOVERNMENT LIBRARY. A library established in a government department or office.

GOVERNMENT PUBLICATION. *See* GOVERNMENT DOCUMENT.

GRADUATE LIBRARY EDUCATION. *See* LIBRARY EDUCATION, GRADUATE.

GRANT-IN-AID. An item of library income deriving from state or federal funds, or an item of state or federal expenditure for subsidies to libraries.

GROSS SQUARE FOOTAGE. The sum of the areas of the library at each floor level included within the principal outside faces at exterior walls, neglecting architectural setbacks or projections.

HEAD LIBRARIAN. *See* LIBRARY DIRECTOR.

HIGH SCHOOL. *See* SCHOOL, FOUR-YEAR HIGH.

HOLDINGS. *See* LIBRARY COLLECTION.

HOURS OF SERVICE. Those hours during the week when a library is open and prepared to render service to its clientele.

INDEXING. The activities included in the preparation—list, card file, or other form—of an array of references to topics, names, or titles in books and periodicals, or to reports, patents, and other nonbook materials.

INFORMATION CENTER. A generic term frequently used to identify a collection of specialized library materials, whether existing as an independent agency or as a division, department, or service within a larger unit. As an independent agency it would constitute a special service, but it would often be listed in a special libraries directory.

INFORMATION CLEARINGHOUSE. A term sometimes applied to a special library which has a limited amount of published material on file, but gathers and relays information by telephone and correspondence and by the use of other libraries.

IN-SERVICE TRAINING. Informal education in librarianship taken by a staff member or student librarian, often consisting of institutes or workshops. Such education usually does not entail college credit but may fulfill certain requirements for certificates. Also called "On-the-job" training.

INSTITUTIONAL LIBRARY. A library maintained by a public or a private institution, such as a prison library, a hospital library.

INTERBORROWING AND INTERLENDING. The practice of borrowing or lending of materials between two administratively independent special libraries in the same establishment.

INTERBRANCH LOAN. A loan of material by one branch library to another.

INTERLENDING. *See* INTERBORROWING AND INTERLENDING.

INTERLIBRARY LOAN. A cooperative arrangement among libraries by which one library may borrow material from another library which is not an integral part of the same system.

INTERLIBRARY REFERENCE SERVICE. A cooperative arrangement among libraries whereby reference work is done by one library for a patron of another library which is not an integral part of the same system.

INTERNAL REPORT. *See* REPORT, INTERNAL.

INTRALIBRARY LOAN. A loan made from one library to another within the same library system.

INVENTORY. A detailed list showing quantities, descriptions, and original cost of library property.

JOURNAL. *See* PERIODICAL.

JUNIOR HIGH SCHOOL. *See* SCHOOL, JUNIOR HIGH.

JUNIOR LIBRARIAN. A staff member doing professional work of a less difficult nature than that of a Senior Librarian (*q.v.*). The Junior Librarian may supervise nonprofessional but not professional staff members.

JUNIOR-SENIOR HIGH SCHOOL. *See* SCHOOL, JUNIOR-SENIOR HIGH.

JUVENILE DEPARTMENT. *See* CHILDREN'S DEPARTMENT.

LEAFLET. *See* NONBOOK MATERIALS; VERTICAL FILE MATERIALS.

LEGISLATIVE MATERIALS. Publications relating to proposed, pending, or completed legislation such as bills and laws; also hearings, reports, and documents on legislative matters by committees of legislative bodies of federal, state, or local governments.

LEGISLATIVE REFERENCE SERVICE. Assistance given by a library to governmental agencies and to a legislature, especially in problems of political administration and in connection with proposed or pending legislation. Within library functions at the state level, such assistance sometimes includes the drafting and indexing of bills.

LIBRARIAN. (1) The head of a library or library system; also known as Chief Librarian, Head Librarian, or Library Director. (2) A professional member of a library staff. (3) Combined with name of department or type of work, the term is used to designate the title of a staff member (e.g., children's librarian; order librarian, etc.).

LIBRARIAN, CERTIFIED. A professional staff member who has been endorsed officially as having met the requirements for employment set by a given state.

LIBRARY. An organized collection of published and other materials with a staff trained to provide and interpret such materials as required to meet the informational, educational and/or recreational needs of a clientele; also its physical facilities.

LIBRARY BOARD. *See* BOARD OF DIRECTORS.

LIBRARY CLASSROOM. A classroom serving as an adjunct to a school library, designed for library instructional uses with groups.

LIBRARY COLLECTION. The total accumulation of all library materials (*q.v.*) provided by a library for its clientele. Also called Library Resources, Library Holdings.

LIBRARY CONSULTANT. An advisor to a librarian, institution, organization, or governmental body, or to a lay group interested in the stimulation, administration, or development of better library services and library buildings and equipment.

LIBRARY DIRECTOR. The head of a library or library system. Also known as Librarian, Chief Librarian, Head Librarian.

LIBRARY DISTRICT. (1) An area designated for subsidies, system activities, or other administrative purposes. (2) An area in which the citizens have voted to assume a tax to support a library.

LIBRARY EDUCATION, GRADUATE. Library education program for which postbaccalaureate library science credit is given by an institution of higher education.

LIBRARY EDUCATION, UNDERGRADUATE. Library education program for which undergraduate credit is given by an institution of higher education.

LIBRARY EXTENSION. *See* EXTENSION OF LIBRARY SERVICE.

LIBRARY HOLDINGS. *See* LIBRARY COLLECTION.

LIBRARY MATERIALS. Those book, periodical, and nonbook items provided by a library for its clientele. This does not include equipment with which to see, hear, or read the items (e.g., projectors, phonographs, readers). *See* BOOK STOCK; NONBOOK MATERIALS; PERIODICALS COLLECTION.

LIBRARY, MULTICOUNTY. *See* MULTICOUNTY LIBRARY.

LIBRARY RESOURCES. *See* LIBRARY COLLECTION.

LIBRARY, SCHOOL. *See* SCHOOL LIBRARY.

LIBRARY SCHOOL. A professional school, department, or division granting a postbaccalaureate degree, and organized and maintained by an institution of higher education for the purpose of preparing students for entrance into the library profession.

LIBRARY SCHOOL, ACCREDITED. A library school approved by the American Library Association, the authorized accrediting agency for programs of library education at the graduate level.

LIBRARY SERVICE. The performance of all activities in a library relating to the collection and organization of library materials and to making the materials and information from them available to a clientele. (A specific aspect of the library's activities may also be described as a service, e.g., Reference Service, Readers' Service.)

LIBRARY, SPECIAL. *See* SPECIAL LIBRARY.

LIBRARY, STATE. *See* STATE LIBRARY.

LIBRARY SYSTEM. (1) An organization based on a plan or procedure in which library units work together, sharing services and resources in a manner which results in improved services to library users. (2) A central library and all of its other service outlets, i.e., branches, deposit stations, bookmobiles.

LIBRARY TRUSTEES. *See* BOARD OF DIRECTORS.

LISTENING AND VIEWING AREA. *See* AUDIO-VISUAL AREA.

LITERATURE SEARCH. A type of reference work which involves extensive scrutiny of indexes and bibliographies, as well as the library's own monographs and periodicals, in order to locate information on the subject of the inquiry.

LOOSE-LEAF SERVICE. A serial publication which is revised, cumulated, and/or indexed by means of new or replacement pages inserted in a loose-leaf binder, and used where latest revisions of information are important, as with legal and scientific material.

MAGAZINE. *See* PERIODICAL.

MAIN LIBRARY. *See* CENTRAL LIBRARY.

MAINTENANCE OF PLANT. Activities necessary to keeping the buildings, grounds, and equipment in operation and in repair.

MAINTENANCE PERSONNEL. Personnel whose duties are concerned with maintenance of plant (*q.v.*), e.g., building engineers, custodians, janitors, guards.

MANUSCRIPT. The handwritten or typewritten copy of an author's work before it is printed.

MAPS. *See* NONBOOK MATERIALS.

MARKET SURVEY. A published study of the potential sales of a new product.

MATERIALS CENTER, SCHOOL SYSTEM. *See* SCHOOL SYSTEM MATERIALS CENTER.

MEMBERSHIP, AVERAGE DAILY. In a given school year, the average daily membership for a given school is the aggregate days membership of the school divided by the number of days school was actually in session. Aggregate days membership is the sum of the days present and absent of all pupils when school was actually in session with pupils under the guidance and direction of teachers in the teaching process.

MICROCARD. An opaque card containing images photographically reduced to a size too small to be read without magnification.

MICROCOPY. *See* MICROFORM.

MICROFICHE. A microfilm sheet containing multiple images in a grid pattern.

MICROFILM. A strip of film containing photographic images usually too small to be read without magnification.

MICROFORM. Any library material which has been photographically reduced in size for storage and protection purposes, and which must be read with the help of enlarging instruments, e.g., microfilm, microcard, microfiche; also called Microcopy and Microtext.

MONOGRAPH. A treatise on a particular subject, usually detailed in treatment but not extensive in scope. It is generally a book or pamphlet, but need not be bibliographically independent.

MULTICOUNTY LIBRARY. A library established by joint action of the governing agencies or by vote of the residents of the counties involved, and governed by a single board of library directors.

MUNICIPAL LIBRARY. A public library established, maintained, and supported through taxation by a city, town, township, borough, village, etc., whose governing board is appointed by the municipal authorities or is elected, or whose library director reports to another arm of the municipal government.

NEWSPAPER. A serial publication issued at stated and frequent intervals (usually daily, weekly, or semiweekly), which reports events and discusses topics of current interest, and is usually a "primary source" of information to its readers.

NONBOOK MATERIALS. Those library materials which do not meet the definition of a book or periodical (*see* BOOK, BOOK STOCK, PERIODICAL, PERIODICALS COLLECTION), such as, audio-visual materials; vertical file materials and similar items which are not individually cataloged; and any other material the form of which requires special handling.

NONPROFESSIONAL PERSONNEL. Library staff members excluding maintenance personnel, but including clerical and similar personnel, who perform under supervision duties requiring special skills and experience, but not a knowledge of the theory of library work.

OFFICE COLLECTION. A convenient, working collection of library materials for the use of an office within the sponsoring agency of a library, but not owned by the library.

OFFPRINT. An impression of an article, chapter, or other portion of a larger work, printed from the type or plates or reproduced from the printed text of the original and separately issued, sometimes with one or more additional pages or leaves.

OPERATING EXPENDITURES. Costs necessary to the rendering of library service, i.e., expenditures for personnel, library materials, binding and supplies, repair or replacement of existing furnishings and equipment, and costs necessary for the maintenance of plant (*q.v.*).

PAMPHLET. An independent publication consisting of a few leaves of printed matter fastened together but not bound; usually enclosed in paper covers. Pamphlets may be included in book stock, periodicals collection, or nonbook material, depending upon their treatment within the library.

PAPERBACK. *See* PAPERBOUND.

PAPERBOUND. A publication bound between paper covers.

PATENT. An official document issued by the United States or another government securing to an inventor, for a term of years, the exclusive right to make, use, and vend his invention.

PERIODICAL. A serial publication which constitutes one issue in a continuous series under the same title, usually published at regular intervals over an indefinite period, individual issues in the series being numbered consecutively or each issue being dated.

PERIODICALS COLLECTION. A library's collection of periodicals, newspapers, and other serials treated like periodicals, whether bound, unbound, or in microform.

PERSONNEL COSTS. A category of library expenditures comprising items relating to the staffing of the library, except those for which the library contracts with an outside party; e.g., salaries and wages before any deductions for social security, hospitalization, retirement.

PHOTOCOPY. A facsimile reproduction of a publication. The term usually applies to copies which are the same size as the original (or slightly reduced in size), as distinguished from microform, which requires enlargement in order to be read.

PHOTOCOPYING. *See* PHOTODUPLICATION.

PHOTODUPLICATION. A service within the library (or operated by the library) for the purpose of preparing photocopies of library material.

PHYSICAL FACILITIES. *See* FACILITIES.

PHYSICAL PLANT. *See* PLANT.

PICTURES, PRINTS, PHOTOGRAPHS. A category of materials comprising *pictorial*, as opposed to *written*, records. *See also* NONBOOK MATERIALS.

PLANT. A library's building (or quarters) with mechanical systems (e.g., heat, light, water) and grounds, but not equipment.

POPULATION SERVED. The number of persons making up a municipality, industrial or governmental establishment, academic community, organization, etc., to which the activities of an individual library are directed; as distinguished from clientele (*q.v.*), which represents the number of persons actually using that library's services.

PRECATALOGED BOOK. A book which is accompanied by catalog cards obtained through purchase, contract, or agreement from a commercial concern or library. *See also* PREPROCESSED BOOK.

PRECATALOGING. The bibliographic searching, usually done before ordering, to establish the correct entry, series, and Library of Congress card order information.

PREPROCESSED BOOK. A book which has been physically prepared for use, obtained through purchase, contract, or agreement from a commercial concern or library. Such physical preparation may include book jacketing, pocketing, stamping, etc. *See also* PRECATALOGED BOOK.

PROFESSIONAL PERSONNEL. The incumbents of professional positions (*q.v.*).

PROFESSIONAL POSITIONS. Those positions in a library which require training and skill in theoretical or scientific parts of the library's work, as distinct from its merely mechanical aspects. Specific examples of professional positions are: Assistant Department Head, Assistant Director, Department Head, Junior Librarian, Library Director, School Librarian, School Library Supervisor, and Senior Librarian.

PUBLIC (SERVICE) AREA. That portion of the reader area (*q.v.*) allocated to public service desks (such as circulation desk, information desk, registration desk), the card catalog, and exhibits and displays.

PUBLIC LIBRARY. A library that serves free all residents of a given community, district, or region, and receives its financial support, in whole or in part, from public funds. In addition to the tax-supported municipal, county, and regional public libraries, this definition includes privately controlled libraries which render, without charge, general library service to a community.

READER AREA. That portion of a library's total floor space allocated for use by the clientele. Rooms having tables and open shelves for the use of readers, and rooms with microform reading devices and audio-visual equipment intended primarily for clientele use, are examples of reader areas.

READERS' ADVISORY SERVICE. Consultation provided for reading problems of adults, recommendations of books and a reading program, and/or instruction in the use of the library and its resources by adults.

READY REFERENCE. Reference work involving questions of a factual nature which can be answered readily, and often for which a special collection of standard reference tools is developed, as distinguished from literature searches.

RECORDINGS. *See* AUDIO-VISUAL MATERIALS; NONBOOK MATERIALS.

REFERENCE DEPARTMENT. The administrative unit in charge of the reference work of a library.

REFERENCE QUESTION. Any request for information or aid which requires the use of one or more sources to determine the answer, or which utilizes the professional judgment of the librarian.

REFERENCE WORK. A library's activity in seeking to locate and supply specific information requested by library users.

REGIONAL BRANCH. A branch library which acts as a more extensive resource center for its clientele, for an area, and/or for a group of smaller units in a library system.

REGIONAL LIBRARY. A library serving a group of communities or several counties and supported in whole or in part by public funds from the governmental units served. *See also* MULTICOUNTY LIBRARY.

REGISTRATION. The process by which persons receive authorization to borrow library materials for use outside the library.

REPAIRING AND MENDING. Restoration and reinforcement of library material, usually performed by members of the library staff, but not involving re-sewing and putting on a new cover (which comes under the heading of rebinding, and is usually performed outside the library by commercial binders).

REPORT. An official or formal record, as of some special investigation, the activities of a corporate body, etc.

REPORT, CLASSIFIED. A technical report whose distribution is limited by security classification regulations of the U.S. Department of Defense.

REPORT, INTERNAL. A report giving details and results of a specific investi-gation by a company for its own research program. Internal reports filed in special libraries are generally confidential within the company and re-stricted for the use of company personnel.

REPORT, TECHNICAL. A report giving details and results of a specific investi-gation of a scientific or technical problem.

REPRINT. A new printing, without material alteration, from new or original type or plates. *See also* OFFPRINT.

RESEARCH LIBRARY. A reference library provided with specialized material, where exhaustive investigation can be carried on in a particular field (as in a technological library) or in several fields (as in a university library).

RESERVE COLLECTION. Library materials which have been removed from the general circulating collection and set aside in an academic library so that they will be on hand for a certain course of study in progress. Usually the circulation and length of loan of items in a reserve collection are restricted so that they will be available to those who have need of them within a limited time period.

RESERVOIR LIBRARY. *See* STORAGE CENTER.

SALARIES. *See* PERSONNEL COSTS.

SALARY RANGE. The lowest and the highest salaries actually paid to incum-bents of a given position classification.

SALARY SCALE. The span in salary, from the lowest to the highest, which has been authorized for a given position classification.

SCHOOL DISTRICT LIBRARY. A free public library established and financially supported by action of a school district for the use of all residents of the district, and supervised by a local board of education or by a separate library board appointed by a board of education.

SCHOOL, ELEMENTARY. A school classified as elementary by state and local practice and composed of any span of grades not above grade eight.

SCHOOL, FOUR-YEAR HIGH. A four-year school immediately following elemen-tary school in an 8-4 plan or, in some instances, a 7-4 plan.

SCHOOL, JUNIOR HIGH. A separately organized and administered secondary school intermediate between elementary and senior high school.

SCHOOL, JUNIOR-SENIOR HIGH. A secondary school organized on a junior-senior basis and administered as a unit under one head.

SCHOOL LIBRARIAN. A librarian certified under state requirements for school librarians, and assigned to service in a school library.

SCHOOL LIBRARIES DEPARTMENT. (1) The administrative unit of a school dis-trict or state agency that supervises libraries in schools and/or has charge of the distribution of books and other reading matter to schools. (2) That administrative unit (also called School Department or Schools Department) of a public library which provides collections and services to pupils and teachers in schools.

SCHOOL LIBRARY. An instruction area specifically designed or adapted for study and reading, and for the custody, circulation, and administration of a collection of materials for the use of the student body, faculty, and school administration.

SCHOOL LIBRARY CONSULTANT. *See* SCHOOL LIBRARY SUPERVISOR.

SCHOOL LIBRARY SPECIALIST. *See* SCHOOL LIBRARY SUPERVISOR.

SCHOOL LIBRARY SUPERVISOR. A school librarian who supervises and coordinates the work of other school librarians of a school system, and provides leadership, guidance, and expertness in school librarianship for the purpose of improving school library service. The terms Director, Consultant, Coordinator, Advisor, Specialist, Head Librarian, and District Librarian are also used to describe this function.

SCHOOL PLANT, COMBINED ELEMENTARY AND SECONDARY. A school plant which houses both an elementary and a secondary school.

SCHOOL, SENIOR HIGH. A secondary school offering the final years of high school work necessary for graduation, and invariably preceded by a junior high school in the same system.

SCHOOL SYSTEM MATERIALS CENTER. A library located in a school system central office which circulates films, filmstrips, recordings, and other audiovisual materials and equipment to the schools of the system.

SEATING CAPACITY. The number of chairs or other seating units available within the library area for the library clientele while they are using library materials.

SENIOR HIGH SCHOOL. *See* SCHOOL, SENIOR HIGH.

SENIOR LIBRARIAN. A staff member doing professional work of a high order of difficulty, for which he is qualified by experience and/or special training. The Senior Librarian may or may not supervise professional staff members, but is not responsible for the administration of a library or a department.

SERIAL. A publication issued in successive parts, usually at regular intervals, and as a rule, intended to be continued indefinitely. Serials include periodicals, newspapers, annuals (reports, yearbooks, etc.), memoirs, proceedings, and transactions of societies; they may include monographic and publishers' series.

SERIAL SERVICE. A serial publication which is revised, cumulated, and/or indexed by means of new or replacement pages (*see* LOOSE-LEAF SERVICE) or cards (*see* CARD SERVICE).

SERVICE AREA. *See* AREA OF SERVICE.

SERVICE-BASED SUBSCRIPTION. Serial subscriptions for which a library is charged according to its income, book fund, circulation, or periodical holdings indexed in the publication on which the subscription is based.

SERVICE OUTLET. Any location where library materials and services are made available to the library's clientele.

SHELF CAPACITY. *See* VOLUME CAPACITY.

SINKING FUNDS. Sums of money set aside or temporarily invested which are pledged for a future expenditure of a specified nature, such as replacement of equipment, new or expanded physical facilities. Sinking funds are part of the unexpended balance of a library's budget.

SLIDES. *See* AUDIO-VISUAL MATERIALS; NONBOOK MATERIALS.

SOUND RECORDINGS. *See* AUDIO-VISUAL MATERIALS; NONBOOK MATERIALS.

SPECIAL COLLECTION. (1) A collection within a library of material of a certain form, on a certain subject, of a certain period or geographical area, or gathered together for some particular reason in a library which is more or less general in character. (2) A branch, division, or department (and sometimes a separate and semi-autonomous unit) of a library system.

SPECIAL LIBRARY. A library maintained by a business firm, association, government agency, or other organized group whose collections are for the most part limited in scope to the subject area of interest to the sponsor.

SPECIAL STUDENT. A student who is not a candidate for a degree, either because he has not met specified requirements for admission to the institution or because he does not wish to be a candidate for a degree.

STAFF. The group of persons who carry on the activities of a library under the direction of the Library Director. *See* MAINTENANCE PERSONNEL; NONPROFESSIONAL PERSONNEL; PROFESSIONAL PERSONNEL.

STANDARD INDUSTRIAL CLASSIFICATION. A coding plan for systematically classifying industrial establishments to secure uniformity and comparability in the presentation of statistical data.

STANDARDS. Objective, observable, and usually quantitative measures of achievement set up as ideals of library service with which a particular library can be compared.

STATE AID. *See* GRANT-IN-AID.

STATE DOCUMENT CENTER. A library that assumes the responsibility of collecting, organizing, and preserving as complete a file as possible of the public documents of the state in which it is located.

STATE LIBRARY. A library maintained by state funds for the use of state officials and employees, and usually for the use of all citizens of the state.

STATE LIBRARY EXTENSION AGENCY. An organization (or a division thereof) created or authorized by a state to promote library service in the state by the establishment, organization, and supervision of public (and sometimes school) libraries. It also assists through counseling and the lending of books and other material to libraries and to communities without libraries. *See also* EXTENSION OF LIBRARY SERVICE.

STATION. *See* DEPOSIT STATION.

STORAGE AREA. That portion of the total floor space of the library building(s) allocated to the storage of materials, supplies, and equipment not in immediate use.

STORAGE CENTER. A library or library agency in which cooperating libraries store little-used books and materials, which are then available on request. Also called Reservoir Library, Deposit Library.

STUDENT ASSISTANT. A student employed part time, usually in the library of a university, college, or school, to perform nontechnical or nonprofessional duties under the supervision of the professional staff; he may be working voluntarily or be paid on an hourly basis.

SUBSCRIPTION. The arrangement by which an organization, a publisher, or an agent provides the library with copies of a periodical, newspaper, or other serial as issued.

SUPPLIES. Material items of an expendable nature that are consumed, worn out, or deteriorate in use.

SURVEY. A scientifically conducted study through which data are gathered according to a definite schedule and are presented in a statistical, tabulated, or summarized form.

TALKING BOOKS. Nonmusical recordings on disc or tape for service to the visually handicapped. *See also* AUDIO-VISUAL MATERIALS.

TAPES. *See* AUDIO-VISUAL MATERIALS.

TEACHING LOAD. The number of course hours assigned to a faculty member.

TEAR SHEET. A sheet torn from a publication; when plural, a clipped article.

TECHNICAL REPORT. *See* REPORT, TECHNICAL.

TECHNICAL SERVICES. Those activities inherent in obtaining, organizing, and preparing the library material for use.

THESIS. An academic dissertation presented by a candidate in partial fulfillment of the requirements for a degree. A thesis constitutes one title but may constitute one or more physical entities.

TITLE. A term used to designate a printed publication which forms a separate whole, whether issued in one or several volumes.

TRADE CATALOG. A publication issued by a manufacturer, a dealer, or a group of manufacturers, describing (and sometimes illustrating) their products, and sometimes including or accompanied by a price list.

TRAINING. *See* IN-SERVICE TRAINING.

TRANSPARENCY. *See* AUDIO-VISUAL MATERIALS.

TRAVELING LIBRARY. A small collection of selected books sent by a central library agency for the use of a branch, group, or community during a limited period.

TRUSTEES. *See* BOARD OF DIRECTORS.

UNDERGRADUATE LIBRARY EDUCATION. *See* LIBRARY EDUCATION, UNDERGRADUATE.

UNEXPENDED BALANCE. That portion of a library's current funds which is not spent and which is pledged toward a particular purpose, such as a sinking fund. Unexpended funds may revert to the appropriating unit or become part of the expendable funds for the succeeding fiscal period.

UNIT COST. A term used in cost accounting to denote the cost of producing a unit of product or rendering a unit of service, e.g., the cost of cataloging a book.

UNIVERSITY LIBRARY. A library, or a system of libraries, established and maintained by a university to meet the needs of its students and faculty.

VERTICAL FILE MATERIALS. Those items such as pamphlets, clippings, pictures, etc., which, because of their shape and often their ephemeral nature, are filed vertically in drawers for ready reference.

VOLUME. For statistical purposes, a volume is a physical unit of any printed, typewritten, handwritten, mimeographed, or processed work contained in one binding or portfolio, hardbound or paperbound, which has been cataloged, classified, and/or made ready for use.

VOLUME CAPACITY. The capacity of a library for storying books (or *volumes*), generally expressed by the total number which can be accommodated on the shelves, or by the total number of linear feet available for housing books and other library materials. Also called Book Capacity or Shelf Capacity.

WEEDING. The selection of library material from the collection to be discarded or transferred to storage.

WITHDRAWAL. The process of removing from library records all entries for a book no longer in the library.

WORK AREA. That portion of a library's total floor space allocated for use by library staff members for performance of their duties. It includes space for desks, furniture, and any needed equipment, as well as space for sorting and packing materials.

WORK WEEK. The number of hours per week that a full-time employee works.

YEARBOOK. *See* ANNUAL.

Appendix A

Persons Attending Regional Conferences

The following persons attended one of the four regional conferences at which the contents of this handbook were discussed. For each conference, the names of those attending (and the library agencies or other organizations at which they are employed) are listed by state. It should be noted that most of the persons in attendance at these regional conferences were also representing national organizations, divisions of the American Library Association, other Associations affiliated with A.L.A., government agencies, or private industry.

ATLANTA, GEORGIA: March 9-10, 1964

Alabama:
Oltman, Florine   Air University, Montgomery

Florida:
Hardaway, Elliott   Univ. of South Florida, Tampa

Georgia:
Anders, Mary Edna   Georgia Inst. of Technology
Austin, Roxanna   State Dept. of Education
Bauer, Charles K.   Lockheed-Georgia Comp.
Blake, Dorothy W.   Atlanta Public Schools
Hagan, Helen   Library School, Emory Univ.
Hightower, Grace   State Dept. of Education
Johnston, Linda M.   Federal Reserve Bank, Atlanta
Jones, Sarah   State Dept. of Education
Jones, U. V.   Law School, Emory Univ.

Kittle, Arthur T.	Georgia Inst. of Technology
LeMay, Geraldine	Savannah Public Schools
McWhorter, Mildred	V. A. Center, Dublin
Nix, Lucile	State Dept. of Education
Reagan, Agnes L.	Library School, Emory Univ.
Rheay, Mary L.	Atlanta Public Library
Sullivan, Sophia	Georgia Inst. of Technology
Taylor, Marion R.	Library School, Emory Univ.
Whitehead, Elizabeth	Fulton County School System

Louisiana:
Brother, Shirley	State Library Agency

Mississippi:
Currier, Lura G.	Library Commission
Langner, Mildred C.	Medical School, Univ. of Mississippi
Schenk, Gretchen K.	Library Commission
Tackett, Evelyn	Library Commission
Vaughn, Esther G.	Library Commission

North Carolina:
Von Oesen, Elaine	State Library Agency

Oklahoma:
Henke, Esther M.	State Library Agency
Hudson, Ralph	State Library Agency
Owens, Virginia	State Library Agency

Tennessee:
Cheney, Frances N.	Peabody Library School, Nashville

Texas:
Jackson, H. Kenneth	State Library Agency

Virginia:
Yoder, Florence B.	State Library Agency

San Francisco, California: March 16-17, 1964

California:
Alma, Sister Mary	Library School, Univ. of San Francisco
Bedsole, Dan	Aerojet General Corp.
Dalton, Phyllis J.	State Library Agency
Durham, Mae J.	Univ. of California, Berkeley
Ferring, Geraldine	San Francisco Public Schls.
Gold, Suzanne	State Library Agency
Griffin, Marjorie	IBM Research Lab.
Holman, W. R.	San Francisco Public Library
Howell, Marvin	State Dept. of Education
Kidman, Roy	Univ. of California, San Diego
Kincaid, Anne	San Francisco Pub. Library
Krushka, Eva	Mills College, Oakland
Marciniak, Lenore	Oakland Library Commission
Mohr, Lucile V.	San Francisco P. L. Commission

Morris, Effie Lee	San Francisco Public Library
Peck, Allan E.	Pomona Public Library
Roth, Elizabeth	Standard Oil of California
Shank, Russell	Univ. of California, Berkeley
Smith, Natalie	State Library Agency
Solomon, Lawrence	Contra Costa County Library
Speed, Bill	Los Angeles Public Library
Stewart, Jack M.	Univ. of California, Berkeley
Thompson, Alleen	General Electric Co., San Jose
Trahan, Marian	Oakland Public Library
Troke, Margaret K.	Stockton Public Library
Warheit, I. A.	IBM, San Jose
Weber, David C.	Stanford Univ. Library
Wight, Edward A.	Library Schl., Univ. of California

Colorado:
Baillie, Stuart	Library Schl., Univ. of Denver
Mott, Larry	State Library Agency

Idaho:
Miller, Helen M.	State Library Agency

Illinois:
Ferguson, Eleanor	American Library Assoc.

Montana:
Longworth, Ruth O.	State Library Commission
Rossiter, W. A.	Dept. of Public Instruction

Nebraska:
Pope, Jane L.	Public Library Commission

Nevada:
Heyer, Mildred J.	State Library Agency
Mauseth, Barbara J.	State Library Agency

North Dakota:
Byrnes, Hazel W.	State Library Agency

Oregon:
Ebert, Eloise Q.	State Library Agency
Fisher, Loretta G.	State Library Agency

Utah:
Davis, Russell	State Library Agency

Washington:
McClaskey, Harris	State Library Agency

Wyoming:
Mortensen, Lee	State Library Agency

CHICAGO, ILLINOIS: March 19-20, 1964

Arkansas:
Neal, Frances	State Library Commission
Schader, Freddy	State Library Commission

Illinois:

Anthony, Louise	Skokie Public Schools
Bailey, George M.	American Library Assoc.
Batchelder, Mildred L.	American Library Assoc.
Boula, James A.	State Dept. of Education
Budington, William A.	John Crerar Library
Claver, Sister Peter	Library School, Rosary College
Corrigan, Dorothy D.	Rockford Public Library
Ennis, Philip H.	Library School, Univ. of Chicago
Fair, Ethel M.	American Library Assoc.
Girolama, Sister M.	Library School, Rosary College
Hertel, Robert R.	Illinois State University
Kelly, Robert Q.	Law Library, De Paul Univ.
Nielander, Ruth	Kemper Insurance
Peterson, Miriam	Library Div., Chicago School System
Poole, Frazer G.	Univ. of Illinois
Ramm, Dorothy V.	Transportation Center Library
Reid, De Lafayette	State Library Agency
Robertson, Giles B.	Univ. of Illinois
Schmidt, Helen	Medical Library Assoc.
Skidmore, Lottie M.	Joliet Junior College Library
Stevenson, Grace	American Library Assoc.
Strable, Edward G.	Walter Thompson Co.
Wildman, Iris J.	Law Library, Northwestern Univ.
Wright, Don	American Library Assoc.
Yast, Helen	American Hospital Assoc.
Yates, Marianne	Transportation Center Library
Yungmeyer, Elinor	Oak Park School System

Indiana:

Banet, Rev. Charles	St. Joseph's College
Sander, Harold J.	Indianapolis Public Library

Iowa:

Bentz, Dale M.	Univ. of Iowa

Michigan:

Booth, Robert	Wayne State Univ.
Carter, Esther	Library Schl., Western Michigan Univ.
Purdy, G. Flint	Wayne State Univ.
Scannell, Francis X.	State Library Agency

Minnesota:

Freeman, Nancy J.	Library Schl., Univ. of Minnesota
Smith, Hannis	State Dept. of Education

Missouri:

Bothe, Edna	State Library Agency
Young, Mrs. Raymond A.	State Library Commission

Ohio:

Jackson, Sidney L.	Library Schl., Kent State Univ.

Texas:
    Hunsberger, W. D.   Texas Women's Univ.

Wisconsin:
    Fuller, Muriel   Library Schl., Univ. of Wisconsin
    Kee, Janice S.   State Library Commission
    Vold, Anna May   Dept. of Public Instruction

NEW YORK CITY, NEW YORK: March 23-24, 1964

Canada:
    Adamson, Edith   Dominion Bureau of Statistics

Connecticut:
    Burgarella, Mary   State Dept. of Education
    Gordon, Harold D.   Univ. of Connecticut

District of Columbia:
    Howard, Paul   Dept. of Interior Library
    Skipper, James M.   Assoc. of Research Libraries

Maryland:
    Graham, Mae   State Dept. of Education
    Taylor, Nettie B.   State Dept. of Education

Massachusetts:
    Harrar, G. A.   Boston Univ. Library
    Leonard, Ruth S.   Library Schl., Simmons College

New Hampshire:
    Allen, Emil W., Jr.   State Library Agency

New Jersey:
    Chirico, Josephine   State Library Agency
    Harlow, Neal   Library Schl., Rutgers Univ.
    Kinder, Katherine L.   Johns-Manville Co.
    Reid, Charles E.   Paramus Public Library
    Roth, Harold   East Orange Public Library
    Seaton, Clare   State Library Agency

New York:
    Bogardus, Janet   Federal Reserve Bank
    Bryan, Alice I.   Library School, Columbia Univ.
    Cummings, Sonya F.   New York City School System
    Gold, Gerald   New York Public Library
    Grech, Anthony P.   New York Bar Assoc.
    Greco, Gloria   College of New Rochelle
    Haas, W. J.   Columbia Univ. Library
    Hacker, Harold   Rochester Public Library
    Keenan, Elizabeth L.   Downstate Medical Center
    Kingery, Robert E.   New York Public Library
    Kinney, Margaret M.   Bronx V. A. Hospital
    Kramer, Esther   New York City School System
    Lukash, Anne   College of New Rochelle
    Mixer, Charles W.   Columbia Univ. Library

Neuberger, Ludwig	Columbia Univ. Law Library
Pautzsch, Richard O.	Brooklyn Public Library
Randall, Gordon E.	IBM Research Library
Richter, Anna J.	R. R. Bowker Co.
Vedder, Marion H.	State Library Agency
Woods, Bill M.	Special Libraries Assoc.

North Carolina:

Carpenter, Ray L.	Library Schl., Univ. of N. C.

Ohio:

Focke, Helen M.	Library Schl., Western Reserve Univ.

Pennsylvania:

Bendix, Dorothy	Library Schl., Drexel Inst. of Tech.
Brown, Margaret C.	Free Library of Philadelphia
Scherer, Henry	Philadelphia Lutheran Seminary
Scudder, Robert E.	Free Library of Philadelphia
Stone, Walter C.	Univ. of Pittsburgh
Woy, Sara	Free Library of Philadelphia

Appendix B

Selected Bibliography

The following selected bibliography represents those works which, in the opinion of the Project Staff, are important amplifications of the various statistical problems that are discussed in the several chapters. Much of the work of this Project was based upon a detailed study of the statistical questionnaires used by the states and the federal government, the advice and consultation of a large number of librarians who worked with the Project, and the personal experience and professional judgment of the Project Staff.

AMERICAN LIBRARY ASSOCIATION. *Definitions for Library Statistics; A Preliminary Draft.* Chicago: The Association, 1961.

ARTANDI, SUSAN. "Special Library Services—Current Thinking and Future Trends," *Special Libraries,* LIV (February, 1963), 103-6.

BONN, GEORGE S. "Implications for the Special Library," *Journal of Education for Librarianship,* II (Spring, 1962), 198-207.

DOWNS, ROBERT B. "Uniform Statistics for Library Holdings," *Library Quarterly,* XVI (January, 1946), 63-9.

————. "Distribution of American Library Resources," *College and Research Libraries,* XVIII (May, 1957), 183-9.

KRUZAS, ANTHONY T. (ed.). *Directory of Special Libraries and Information Centers.* Detroit: Gale Research Co., 1963.

LEIGH, ROBERT D. *The Public Library in the United States.* New York: Columbia University Press, 1950.

LYLE, GUY R. "Counting Library Holdings," *College and Research Libraries,* XI (January, 1950), 69-72.

MORLEY, LINDA H. *Contributions Toward a Special Library Glossary.* New York: Special Libraries Association, 1950.

ROGERS, RUTHERFORD D. "Measurement and Evaluation," *Library Trends,* III (October, 1954), 177-87.

SCHICK, FRANK L. (ed.). "The Future of Library Service: Demographic Aspects and Implications (Part I)," *Library Trends,* X (July, 1961), 1-70.

———. "The Future of Library Service: Demographic Aspects and Implications (Part II)," *Library Trends,* X (October, 1961), 71-283.

TAUBER, MAURICE F., and ASSOCIATES. *Technical Services in Libraries.* New York: Columbia University Press, 1954.

THOMPSON, ELIZABETH H. *A.L.A. Glossary of Library Terms.* Chicago: American Library Association, 1943.

TURNER, MARY C. *The Bookman's Glossary.* 4th ed. New York: R. R. Bowker Co., 1961.

U.S. DEPARTMENT OF HEALTH, EDUCATION, AND WELFARE, *Office of Education (No. OE 15022). Statistics of Libraries—An Annotated Bibliography of Recurring Surveys.* Washington, D.C.: The Office, 1961.

WHEELER, JOSEPH L., and GOLDHOR, HERBERT. *Practical Administration of Public Libraries.* New York: Harper and Row, 1962.

WIGHT, EDWARD A. *Public Library Finance and Accounting.* Chicago: American Library Association, 1943.

WILSON, LOUIS R., and TAUBER, MAURICE F. *The University Library.* New York: Columbia University Press, 1956.

WRIGHT, J. E. "The Special Library and Information Service." (In ASHWORTH, WILFRED. *Handbook of Special Librarianship and Information Work.* London, ASLIB, 1955, pp. 1-9.)

Index

NOTE. This index includes references only to Chapters I-VII in this handbook. The glossary should be consulted for definitions of terms as necessary. Statistics common to more than one type of library are listed under the subject rather than under the types of libraries.